**THE PROPER CARE OF
BUDGIES
TW-104**

Photo credits: Dr. Herbert R. Axelrod, Darlene Campbell, Penny Corbett, Kerry V. Donnelly, Michael De Freitas, Michael Gilroy, Harry V. Lacey, Stephanie Logue, Susan C. Miller, Ron and Val Moat, H. Reinhard, L. Robinson, San Diego Zoo, Vincent Serbin, Louise Van der Meid, Norma Veitch, Vogelpark Walsrode, Wayne Wallace.

Drawings: John R. Quinn, M. Shipman.

Distributed in the UNITED STATES by T.F.H. Publications, Inc., One T.F.H. Plaza, Neptune City, NJ 07753; in CANADA to the Pet Trade by H & L Pet Supplies Inc., 27 Kingston Crescent, Kitchener, Ontario N2B 2T6; Rolf C. Hagen Ltd., 3225 Sartelon Street, Montreal 382 Quebec; in CANADA to the Book Trade by Macmillan of Canada (A Division of Canada Publishing Corporation), 164 Commander Boulevard, Agincourt, Ontario M1S 3C7; in ENGLAND by T.F.H. Publications, PO Box 15, Waterlooville PO7 6BQ; in AUSTRALIA AND THE SOUTH PACIFIC by T.F.H. (Australia) Pty. Ltd., Box 149, Brookvale 2100 N.S.W., Australia; in NEW ZEALAND by Ross Haines & Son, Ltd., 82 D Elizabeth Knox Place, Panmure, Auckland, New Zealand; in the PHILIPPINES by Bio-Research, 5 Lippay Street, San Lorenzo Village, Makati, Rizal; in SOUTH AFRICA by Multipet Pty. Ltd., P.O. Box 35347, Northway, 4065, South Africa. Published by T.F.H. Publications, Inc. Manufactured in the United States of America by T.F.H. Publications, Inc.

The Proper Care of
BUDGIES

Dennis Kelsey-Wood

Contents

Facing page: It is not surprising that the budgerigar holds the title of most popular pet bird. It is attractive, hardy, and easy to breed.

Introduction

The budgerigar, or parakeet, as it is still often referred to in the USA, is the world's most numerous and popular pet bird. It is also the most popular exhibition bird and the bird that is available in the widest range of color forms. To add to its impressive credentials, it can be taught to mimic many words, is a hardy parrot, and is a ready and willing breeder. Finally, it remains the least expensive of any parrot species.

Parrots were known in Europe for a few centuries before the budgerigar first arrived, but they were largely the preserve of the wealthy. The working class kept pigeons or small

finches, and as the years passed the canary became the most popular cage bird available. In 1840 the English naturalist and artist John Gould returned to England from Australia with live specimens of the 'budgie' and these aroused much interest. Somewhat later in London two ships docked that contained a very large consignment of budgerigars — a few thousand in fact. These were quickly snapped up by a well-known animal dealer of the time and were quickly sold at a handsome profit.

Further ships landed in England and in the ports of mainland Europe, with increasing frequency, so a healthy trade developed. However, it was not long before breeders realized

these little parrots were hardy enough to breed very well in the temperate climates of Europe. A good-sized industry resulted based around large commercial breeding units. These were not able to survive for too long because backyard breeders were also able to produce many birds at competitive prices. With the passage of a few more years the large profits from the sale of budgies quickly fell as the supply ran ahead of demand.

The budgie needed some extra impetus and this arrived in the form of the light yellow mutation in 1872. Just six or seven years later the blue mutation appeared. Budgies were really back in business because this opened up a whole new area of interest — color breeding. Six more colors had emerged by the time the Budgerigar Club

Facing page: This colorful, small parrot is a lovebird. Lovebirds are not tamed as easily as are budgies and are aggressive towards other kinds of birds.

(now the Budgerigar Society, UK) came into being. This club was to give the species tremendous promotion, and steadily the charming little budgie was beginning to chase after the canary as the sweetheart of the bird world.

Today, the budgerigar's numbers are vastly greater than those of the canary, and it is unlikely that any other bird will challenge the position of the budgerigar for many years to come. Indeed, so numerous are budgerigars that they are no longer seen on many of the dealer lists in avicultural magazines. The price of the birds has not kept pace with the increased costs of keeping them on lists. However, a quality exhibition specimen can still change hands for a very substantial fee. There is little doubt that for the first time birdkeeper, or breeder,

Budgies are an ideal choice for the beginner hobbyist.

A natural perch will be much enjoyed by your budgie, and the variations in its thickness will provide for good exercise and conditioning of the bird's claws.

the budgerigar has to be the finest choice. It is a fully domesticated species. Although for many years budgies could still be imported from Australia, this came to an end over thirty years ago when the Australian government placed a ban on the export of its flora and fauna, which persists to this day. This means that all budgerigars outside of that country are bred from domestic sources — so in owning budgerigars you are not taking any birds from their wild habitat.

The potential number of colors and their combinations available to you is vast, and there is even a choice of three crested varieties. In the coming years it is quite possible that more color mutations will appear; maybe even an all-black budgerigar will appear. This would create terrific interest and a good deal of cash for its owner. A red budgie was imported into England just after World War II and this caused considerable interest, no doubt changing hands for a princely sum. Alas, when it went through its next molt it turned out to be a white bird that had been skillfully dyed by its Asiatic owner!

Within this volume it is hoped you will find all of the information you could possibly need to make a start with these delightful parakeets. It will provide you with a complete base on which to advance your knowledge, both by practical experience and by referral to other detailed works, many of which have been published over the years.

Facing page: If you keep a pair of budgies, it is likely that the birds will bond more closely with each other than with you.

Natural History

The budgerigar, which has the scientific name of *Melopsittacus undulatus*, is native to Australia (but absent from Tasmania).It is an introduced species in Florida, where captive stock that escaped has established colonies.

Its area of distribution in Australia is equaled only by the cockatiel (*Nymphicus hollandicus*) and the Galah cockatoo (*Eolophus rosiecapillus*). It is generally absent from the coastline, especially that of the east, and the Cape York Peninsula. It is found in scrub, open and timbered grasslands, and timbered areas near watercourses. It is nomadic, moving in vast flocks in search of water and seeding grasses. The size of the flocks can number into many thousands and have been known to almost blot out the sun as they pass overhead.

Their movement is swift and precise. They are most active in the early morning and late afternoon before the sun reaches its most penetrating heat. At this time they will retreat to the sparse shade of whatever trees and shrubs are in the vicinity. They breed during the warmer Australian months — which are August to January, though they are variable in this depending on when the rains appear. This triggers reproduction because it results in the sudden appearance of a whole range of wild plants and much insect activity. Both are useful in rearing the chicks. In seasons of drought, thousands of these birds

Not unlike other kinds of pets, the more time you spend with your budgerigar, the more it will become accustomed to your company. Once you have won your budgie's trust, it will be relatively easy to tame and train him.

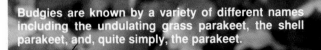

Budgies are known by a variety of different names including the undulating grass parakeet, the shell parakeet, and, quite simply, the parakeet.

will perish through lack of water, and at such times they will not breed.

DESCRIPTION

The budgerigar hardly needs describing as it is so well known. Suffice to say that the wild type (referred to genetically as normal) is a basically green bird with a yellow forehead and face. A series of black spots (usually six) adorn the throat, whilst some of the cheek feathers are tipped with violet blue. The nape and wings are barred with black and yellow. The underside of the tail is a green-blue. The cere — the fleshy area surrounding the nostrils — is blue in the male and brown in the female. The legs are a gray brown and the eye color is a dark brown with a yellow to white iris surrounding this. The bill is basically horn colored but may be suffused

The budgerigar (*Melopsittacus undulatus*) is native to Australia. This attractive pair of budgies illustrates just several of the various color varieties in which these birds are available.

One of the best known budgerigar color varieties, the green, is shown here.
The yellow areas provide a nice contrast in the bird's overall appearance.

Facing page: Artist's rendering of a normal green budgerigar. **Above:** These youngsters are all from a single nest. To many budgie keepers, color breeding is one of the most exciting aspects of the hobby.

with gray and blue.

Immatures are duller in color than the adults, have the barring of the neck extending over the crown. They lack the eye ring, which develops as the birds reach about three months of age. Their throat spots are smaller and less circular. The juveniles molt into adult plumage when they are about four or five months old, after which time it is difficult to assess the age of the birds (but in captivity this can be determined if the birds carry a closed ring that is dated). The color of the bill (beak) in immatures appears a bluish pink color but should not be taken as a guide to sex as both sexes have this color.

CALL NOTES

These range from a soft warbling sound to a disyllabic chatter to a sort of screech when frightened. The sound of a budgerigar is not offensive, though large numbers of them can be heard some distance away and in the wild they are often heard before they are seen.

COMMON NAMES

The name budgerigar is thought to have its derivation in the Aboriginal term of Betcherrygah, meaning good eating. We must therefore assume this little parrot was one of the culinary delights of these native peoples, which would not be surprising. Other names applied to the budgie are shell parrot, warbling grass parrot (parakeet), zebra parrot, canary parrot, scalloped parrot, and Australian lovebird. These have now largely been dropped other than in a few local regions in Australia. As mentioned in the introduction, the term parakeet lingers on in the USA, but as it is a term that can be applied to very many parrots its use is vague and will no doubt fall into disuse, as it is already doing.

CLASSIFICATION OF THE BUDGERIGAR

The budgerigar is a member of the large group of birds known as parrots. All share certain and obvious external features such as a hooked beak. They are often characterized by gaudy coloration. There are about 350 species to be found around the world, with the two main areas of distribution being South America and Australasia. The terms parakeets and parrots are loose terms, but

The British ornithologist John Gould is credited with introducing the budgerigar into Great Britain in 1840. Since that time, the budgie has become a popular pet bird worldwide.

The budgie's small size makes it easy to care for and accommodate—even in the smallest of apartments.

hook bills is also occasionally used for these birds. The nearest relatives to parrots are thought to be pigeons and doves.

The scientific classification of the parrots is given in the following chart. It may be found that in other works it will differ slightly because differing taxonomists are not always able to agree on the value of certain features. Under the rules of classification they are within their rights to present their own classification, so it is a case of favoring one or other of those presented. The one cited here is from Howard and Moore in *A Complete Checklist of the Birds of The World*, 1984.

The species is monotypic meaning there are no other species within this genus. There are also no known geographic variations.

generally the species with short tails are called parrots and those with long ones are called parakeets. The term

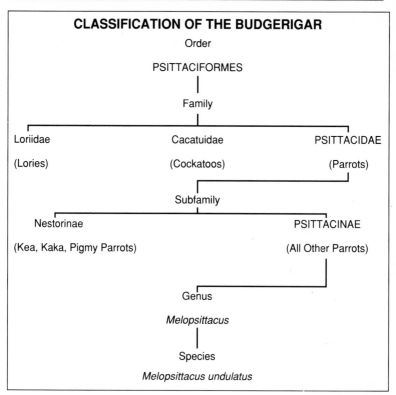

CLASSIFICATION OF THE BUDGERIGAR

Order

PSITTACIFORMES

Family

Loriidae	Cacatuidae	PSITTACIDAE
(Lories)	(Cockatoos)	(Parrots)

Subfamily

Nestorinae	PSITTACINAE
(Kea, Kaka, Pigmy Parrots)	(All Other Parrots)

Genus

Melopsittacus

Species

Melopsittacus undulatus

SCIENTIFIC NOMENCLATURE

Many birdkeepers, indeed many breeders, do not understand why scientific names of birds and other animals are always in Latin, so you may find the explanation of interest. By just looking at the list of common names applied to budgerigars it is at once apparent that two people could be talking about the same bird yet not realize this. The problem becomes magnified when you consider that in all languages there will be a common name for the bird.

Because of this, a system that would be international in its application was devised in the 18th century by a Swedish naturalist, Carolus Linnaeus. It has of course been much streamlined over the years but essentially retains the original fundamentals. Latin was the chosen language both because it was a dead language, thus more acceptable than English or French or whichever, to all countries, and because it was already the language of scholars.

The system is called the Binomial (or Binominal) System of Nomenclature and is based around the fact that every species of plant and animal has its own unique name. This is comprised of two parts. The first is the generic (genus) name and the second is the specific or trivial name. There may be one or any number of species in a genus, but each will have its own trivial name, so it is uniquely identifiable. Every country in the world recognizes the system, so there is never any confusion over which organism is being referred to.

The generic name is always commenced with a capital letter, the trivial always with a lowercase. The species name is thus only given by the use of this binomial. It is standard practice to always place the species name, or the genus if used by itself, in a typeface differing from that of the text. This invariably means it will appear in italic. The entire system is controlled by an extremely complex set of rules and is a fascinating study in its own right.

Normal colored budgies are less expensive than "fancy" colored birds—those in various shades and combinations of blues, grays, whites, and violets.

It is not a static system as is sometimes thought. When new information comes to light on a species, this may mean a given animal, or a whole group of animals, have to be reclassified in light of this information. The system brings together the sum total knowledge of a species, a genus, a family and all groups (ranks) within the system, at any given point in time. This is why some animals are seen under differing scientific names in older books — but even this is catered for so that this fact can be indicated in the new name until such time as it is appreciated that a change has taken place.

The budgerigar is monotypic, but were another good species of it to be discovered then this creates the need to form a trinomial. What would happen is that the first species identified would have its trivial name repeated and the new species would receive its own trivial trinomial. The species *M. undulatus* would thus be made up of two subspecies, *M. undulatus undulatus* and *M. undulatus albifrons* (if the new type had a white front for example).

Regardless of how many subsequent subspecies were discovered, you would always be able to identify the first species so named because of its repeated trivial. This original form is often referred to as the nominate race. It is typical of the type, which is not to say it is typical of the species, because it may be found that it is actually not the most typical of that species. You may often see a date following the name of a species, which indicates when it was first named.

To be successful in the keeping of budgerigars, you should know as much as possible about the habits and needs of these birds. TFH Publications offers a number of books about budgies for both novice and experienced hobbyists.

Housing for budgies varies from one region to another. This illustration
depicts one type of budgie housing that is used in China.

Cages and Aviaries

Having made your decision to obtain one or a number of budgerigars, your thoughts should turn to the way in which they are to be accommodated. This should be given a great deal of consideration, especially if you plan to have aviaries and a birdroom. Even the pet owner could provide much better accommodation for his pet if he were prepared to think beyond the usual cage sold for these pet birds. In this chapter we can look at the many aspects of providing budgerigars with suitable homes and the furnishings such accommodation will require.

CAGES

Cages can be broadly divided between those used by pet owners and those preferred by breeders. The largest units that might be called a cage might also be regarded as an indoor flight: the two terms are really only a question of size. For many years breeders preferred wooden cages with wire fronts, whereas pet owners obtained all-wire cages made specifically for budgies. There has been a shift in thinking over the years and many of today's breeders have all-wire cages, albeit larger than those used for pets, and with a more utilitarian design.

THE COMMERCIAL BUDGERIGAR CAGE

This has remained largely unchanged over the years, it being a case that furnishings have been updated and some redesigning is evident in the cage itself.

The main requirements for a budgerigar cage are that it should be as large as possible and uncluttered so that it allows the bird the maximum room in which to exercise. Length is far more important than height, so the fashionable tall round cages are of little value to any bird. Visit a number of pet stores so that you can see a wide range of designs. Most will be chromium plated, but you can obtain them with epoxy resin finishes that are available in a number of colors, thus allowing you to coordinate them with your room. Owners in the USA are possibly better catered for than those in other countries, as the range of cages is enormous, culminating in the tailor-made units.

Whatever the cost of the cage it should feature certain basic requirements. There should be no protruding or poorly finished bars or pieces of metal that might be injurious to the bird. The bars should be well chromed or otherwise covered so there are no areas of bare metal that might quickly rust and become a health hazard. Those with removable plastic bases, rather than those in metal, are easier to keep clean. Some have spring-loaded doors whilst others have clips to hold the door closed. I think the latter are the better proposition because you can place your hands into the cage much easier rather than if it is closing on your arm all the time.

The better models will have built-in landing platforms. The number of perches included will normally be two or three

All-wire cages are sturdy, durable, and easily transportable. Your local pet shop carries a variety of budgie cages from which you can choose.

and these should be made of wood. If they feature plastic perches, I would throw these away and obtain replacements in doweling or natural tree branches, such as willow or apple. These can be wedged between the bars, or you can purchase perch holders from your bird or pet store. Plastic perches are not good for the feet of budgerigars because the plastic sweats and can cause the bird's feet to become sore.

Your budgie will prefer natural branches the most because these offer variable thicknesses along their length. This makes for good foot exercise, and they can nibble away at the bark, which is good for their beak. The perches are easily replaced once your pet has stripped the bark from the branch. Open pot feeders are often included in cages. These can be left in place for fruits and grit, because

Natural perches are fine for use by budgerigars, but be sure that they have not been chemically treated in any way.

you will find it more convenient to use self-dispensing seed and water pots — of which there are many styles to choose from.

Budgie cages may be fitted with elasticized plastic covers around their base in order to stop seed from falling out, or they may have glass or plastic panels that slide into grooves, or they may be of the all-plastic-base type, which can be detached from the cage part of the unit. A more modern approach is to fit rigid plastic aprons that return spilt seed back onto the cage floor, along with any falling feathers and other debris. It is then removed via the sliding floor tray. These aprons can be purchased as separate units.

The range

A cage such as this is fine for transporting your budgie, but the bird's permanent home should provide much more space.

of toys for budgies is considerable, but do not over fill the cage with these as is sometimes seen. A swing and maybe a ladder is really all that is needed — along with twigs that the bird will enjoy chewing on. Some cages come complete with stands, but these are not always very stable. Tripod types and those that have large rings to hang the cage from are easily toppled over, in spite of the fact that some are weighted at the base. A better

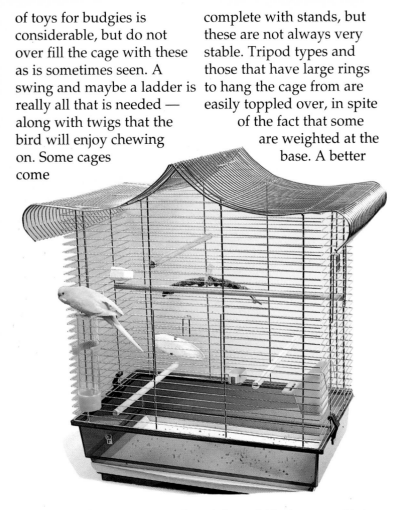

A well-appointed budgie cage. Especially useful is the removable tray, which can easily be cleaned and disinfected.

idea is to place the cage on a solid base, such as a table or other unit.

BREEDER CAGES

These come in two basic styles, the wood and the all-metal. They can be purchased individually or they are available in doubles, triples, tiers, indeed all manner of combinations to suit individual needs. The size and quality of their construction is equally variable. You can even purchase panels of weldwire, with which you can assemble your own cages. Budgerigar cage fronts can be purchased, and you can thus make your own breeder/stock cages in sizes to fit the available space. Double breeder cages are the best investment because these will have removable sliding partitions in them. This will allow you to separate stock as required, or to remove the partition and have a large flight cage.

The wooden box cages are actually better for keeping pet birds in because they offer much more room than the standard budgie cage. A good size would be 122x45x45cm (48x18x18in), which would give the bird the opportunity to at least stretch its wings as it flew from one end to the other. You can purchase the cages in unpainted wood and paint these to your favored color. The inside is best in a light pastel shade — use an emulsion or a lead-free gloss. If you make your own box cage, include a removable sliding tray so you can clean the cage easily. Do be sure to purchase budgie fronts and not those for finches. The two differ in the design of the door and in width between the bars.

A variation on the standard box cage is to have wire fronts on two sides — either along the lengths, or on one length and one end. These offer more security for the bird than the all-wire

When you make your cage selection is the ideal time to purchase those items—perches and the like—that your pet will need in his home.

cage yet still enable the bird to see what is going on around it. The perches can be placed a very short distance in from each end to facilitate the maximum flying space.

The all-wire breeding

Travel can be an upsetting experience for your little feathered friend. When you bring him home, put him in a nice quiet area.

Not uncommonly, a tame budgie will position himself on the shoulder of his favorite person to get a bird's eye view of things.

cage has become much more popular in recent years because it provides fewer places for parasites to hide, and also meets the needs of the birds better. Budgerigars are very gregarious. When breeding they like to both hear and see their fellows. This induces them to go about the business of breeding more readily. The drawback to such units is that there tends to be more dust and feathers falling to the floor, so you must be very methodical in ensuring cleaning is done daily.

If you have blocks of breeding cages, you should place these onto legs so the bottom cages are well above floor level. This will be better for the birds and will enable you to sweep under the cages to get at all the debris. An even better idea is to have the blocks of cages mounted on castors so they can easily be moved. Many commercial block units come complete with castors. Pet shops invariably sell single or double breeder cages, but if you want blocks of cages you will need to contact a specialist supplier. These advertise in the avicultural magazines. The latter are well recommended because they carry many adverts for specialized bird equipment, as well as for birds, and articles on these.

INDOOR FLIGHTS

The indoor flight is the perfect alternative to the cage. It allows for more birds to be kept and gives them far greater room to move around in. Most breeders will have some indoor flights, often attached to the aviary flights, but more and more pet owners are also owning these. Again, you can purchase commercial flights that come in a range of sizes and styles, or you can assemble your own to fit in a given room or space. They could be the walk-in type or those that are raised from the ground to provide storage space underneath.

You may have a large alcove that is a natural for a flight cage because it may only need a front to complete the basic unit. You may wish to feature a flight on a balcony, or even to use a spare room as a large indoor flight. The possibilities are limited only by your own imagination.

As with blocks of cages, a number of commercial indoor flights have castors fitted to them, a very useful idea because they are easily moved from one location (or even home) to another. Such a home unit can be taken onto the balcony on those warm summer days, yet can easily be taken indoors if the weather turns for the worse.

If you decide to design your own, you are advised to purchase 19G weldwire with a hole size of 2.5x1.25 (1x1/2in). The gauge (G) is the thickness of the wire and it is available in many numbers — the lower the number the thicker the wire. Weldwire is altogether better than chicken coop mesh because it is more rigid and will last far longer. You can choose from galvanized wire or that which is coated with green or black plastic. The latter is more expensive but does look nice.

You can purchase weldwire in numerous hole sizes. The dimension given is best for budgerigars, as it is small enough to ensure that mice or other unwanted visitors cannot get into the cage. This is important in birdrooms, but for pet birds in the home you could cut costs and use a hole size of 2.5x2.5cm (1x1in). Weldwire is sold in various widths. Shop around to find that best suited to the design you are planning (or design the flight to take account of the most readily available size). As an alternative to making

A finger-tame budgerigar is a true delight to its owner. If this is your goal with your pet, remember that time and patience are essential to your success in this regard.

your own framework, you can purchase ready assembled panels and need only screw these together.

Doors are also available ready made so you have lots of options these days.

If you are making your

own 'walk in' flight cage(s), be sure that you feature an easy-to-clean floor. Consider also whether the lighting is to be internal or external. In the latter instance there is no problem, but in the former you must be sure there is no chance that the birds could nibble on any exposed wiring, which would really give them a shock! In order to restrict seed and feathers falling out of the cage and onto the floor, it is best to fashion an apron on all

Below: An assortment of variously colored budgies. **Facing page:** A lutino budgerigar.

exposed wire.

If you make your own wooden framework (and even on those purchased as assembled units), be sure that the cut ends of the weldwire are covered so there is no risk that a budgerigar could injure itself on this. Budgies wearing closed rings are especially vulnerable in this respect. You can fix a piece of wooden battening over the edges that have been stapled down. Better still, use rigid plastic and screw it over the edging. Budgerigars tend to nibble on exposed wood, but will generally ignore plastic, so it will not look unsightly due to the activities of the birds. Do remember that if you have an indoor flight for your pet budgerigars you cannot include plants in it because they would soon be destroyed by the birds. You may be able to feature some artificial plants, or you could use plants just outside of the flight to make it more attractive. Likewise, a home flight might feature a mural along the back. There are many panoramas to select from and they can be extremely effective. Place the natural branch perches such that the birds cannot reach the edges of the mural, otherwise they will start to peel it off!

AVIARIES

There is little doubt that the best way to keep budgerigars is in an aviary. In these they are able to live an outdoor life, albeit a confined one, and enjoy the benefits of the sunshine, the breezes, the showers and the ability to fly around as they wish, and in the company of their own kind. Just how good life is for them will be determined by the effort and cost their owner has placed into the design and construction of the aviary. The latter can never be too big.

There are basically two types of aviary owner: the uniform style, often rather utilitarian to look at, and designed for ease of management. The mixed collection owner will often put more thought into the

specialist budgerigar breeder and the mixed collection owner/breeder. The former tend also to be exhibitors. In general, their aviaries are invariably of

A good location for your budgie's cage is a room that is draft-free, of moderate temperature (not the kitchen!), and allows the bird to observe family activities.

A well-stocked aviary. It is not that uncommon for a hobbyist to start out with just a pair of birds, only to get so caught up in the hobby that he winds up with a collection like this!

esthetic beauty of the aviary, because such owners may only have a small number of flights, and the beauty of the aviary is often, to them, a major part of the attraction of being a birdkeeper. With a little forethought, the two types can be brought together to provide aviaries that are very practical to manage, yet extremely pleasing on the eye.

INITIAL CONSIDERATIONS

Before setting about the task of erecting an aviary, it is always prudent to devote quite a bit of time to planning the project. All too often, in a surge of enthusiasm, beginners will quickly build or purchase an aviary only to find it is totally inadequate for their purposes a few months later. Let us look at a few of the things that should be pondered before anything is

put in hand. These will apply regardless of whether you are thinking in terms of one or two aviaries or a whole run of them.

1. The legal aspect. You should not assume that you can always erect aviaries in your garden. There may be

Keeping one or several budgies in your home is generally not subject to regulation by your local governing body. However, if you plan to keep these birds on a large scale, you should check local laws regarding the keeping of livestock.

bylaws in your locality that restrict what you can and cannot keep where livestock is concerned. The restriction may limit the number of birds you can keep, or the type of building they are housed in. For example, portable aviaries may be acceptable — brick units may require building permits. Houses near commercial bird quarantine stations may be very restricted where aviary birds are concerned. Check with your local authority. It is also wise to discuss the matter with your immediate neighbors, who might have visions of raucous macaws screeching throughout the day. They may be worried that your aviaries may attract rats, snakes, or birds of prey. If they are informed of your plans, they are less likely to feel you have shown them no consideration, thus less likely to have objections.

2. How many? You will obviously have an idea of how many aviaries you plan to start off with. Give some thought to future expansion if you get really hooked on breeding. This might suggest that your initial site may not be the best one because it allows no room for extensions.

3. The site. This is a most important consideration. It may be that you have little choice in the matter, so must overcome any problems this creates. However, if a choice is open to you then consider the following points. Avoid placing aviaries under trees, as these present many problems. They attract flies in the summer and are very damp places in the winter. They restrict the amount of sunshine that enters the flights, and wild birds will be continually dropping fecal matter into the flight,

or on its roof if it is covered. There will be leaves falling in autumn, which means more work for you. Rainwater will be dripping into the flights long after the rain has stopped. Finally, the roots from trees may start to push up any concrete or paving floors you may have in the flights.

Avoid very low spots in a garden. These may drain after heavy rains and create a problem in the flights or birdroom: dampness. Clearly, you must not place aviaries over sewage inspection pits or above electrical or water mains. Inspect your house plans to see where these are located. It is wise to have the aviaries where you can see them easily from your house. Apart from watching the birds, this makes good security sense. Sadly, the number of thefts from aviaries rises each year.

Today's budgerigar cages are notably sophisticated in their design. The one shown here features a self-attached bird bath.

If possible, you will want a site that faces south or south-east (the reverse in Australia). This is so the birds are both protected from north and westerly winds, and also so they enjoy the benefit of the early morning sunshine. Finally, consider the distance from utilities, as the chances are you will wish to avail yourself of these. Electric, water and sewage are very handy to have in your birdroom; they will make the day-to-day chores far less unappealing and will make doing them much more comfortable as well, especially in the cold winter months.

Adequate perch space should be available for all of your budgies. Make certain that they are not overcrowded, as this can make them nervous.

THE COST

Most of us are restricted in what we might like to do by the cost of things. Ideally, the best advice is to purchase the finest materials and plan for maximum size of both flights and birdroom. You do not actually have to include a birdroom in your plans, but this is certainly to be recommended for all but those who live in year-round sunny climates. Even the latter will find such a building of practical value, so I will assume you want one.

It is much wiser to have a few really nice aviaries than a larger number of lesser quality units that represent a compromise dictated by cost. It simply means you must stagger your project over two or more seasons. This is sound policy anyway. The costs should include featuring a good solid floor, not bare earth which is a decided health hazard. Although double netting is not needed between adjacent budgerigar flights, I would suggest you cost and plan for this. The reason is because you may at a later date decide to include lovebirds, ringnecks, or other parrots in your collection. These will need such netting, as they often try to bite the feet of birds landing on any common netting separating them from other birds.

You should include in your costs the price of certain equipment, such as heaters, coolers, and ionizers. When your design is completed, shop around a number of suppliers, as you will find quite a variation in the prices you are quoted for the same materials. In preparing your plans and costing them, you will need

Don't skimp when it comes to accommodating your budgie. A well-cared-for pet is a happy pet.

to know what should be considered the essentials of an aviary with an adjoining birdroom, and what furnishings and equipment are needed.

THE AVIARY FLOOR

Although a bare earth or grass floor would seem an ideal base for an aviary, the reality is quite the reverse. Grass will not last long with budgerigars and in any case is a bad surface. The constant droppings of the budgies, together with those of wild birds, means the earth will quickly become a breeding ground for pathogenic bacteria. Further, rodents, and even foxes, might burrow into it.

The least expensive option would be to cover the earth floor with a few centimeters of gravel (at least ten). The few weeds that manage to grow through will soon be eaten by the birds. You can hose and rake the gravel to wash away fecal matter, but small feathers are less easily removed. As it is not the easiest of material to walk on, you could lay some paving (garden) slabs to create a pathway. Such slabs could be used to cover the entire aviary. They are easier to keep clean than gravel and offer greater protection against burrowing animals. They are available in a number of shapes and colors, so you could make an interesting design — or settle for a plain covering. Lay them on a bed of brick rubble covered with sand, the latter allowing you to ensure that a nice level surface is formed — level but sloping away from the birdroom.

Concrete is clearly the best surface if viewed in terms of its ability to be washed down. It is not the

The area in which you choose to house your budgie should not be subject to extreme fluctuations in temperature.

most attractive covering, but you can mix coloring powders into the concrete mix. Alternatively, you could apply concrete paint, maybe green, to give it greater esthetic appeal. Be sure it is of a good depth (min 10cm), otherwise it will crack during freezing weather. It should be laid during the spring or autumn, when it can dry out slowly. In the heat of the summer, it will dry too quickly unless constantly wetted with sacking or spraying. In order to give it greater strength, you can lay sheets of 2.5cm-hole-size weldwire at about the half-thickness level. You can support the weldwire on strategically placed bricks so it does not sink into the wet concrete.

Extend the concrete base beyond the planned perimeter of the aviary. This will provide a walkway or a good base on which to lay slabs. You could, of course, lay slabs onto the concrete in the aviary, if you wish, to create a more attractive finish. The aviary floor should slope away from the birdroom or shelter so that rain and hosed water are carried away. You can add a runaway channel along the far end of the flight so the water is carried out of the aviary into a soakaway. A plastic pipe can lead it through the aviary wall (or whatever forms the perimeter). Use a good-sized pipe so it will easily cope with whatever water is likely to need draining. Cover the pipe with a suitable weldwire mesh so the budgies can't walk out of the aviary and rodents or snakes cannot get in.

THE AVIARY PERIMETER WALL

You can fix your aviary weldwire panels directly onto the concrete base, or

Budgies are notorious for their proclivity to gnaw on just about anything, so exercise caution in what items your budgie has access to.

choice, the panels are screwed to the base with framefixer screw kits. Alternatively, you can drill a hole in the base and then insert a good-sized bolt into this head down. Cement this in — having used a bolt long enough such that it will pass through the wood leaving enough exposed shank to be tightened down with a nut.

THE AVIARY PANELS

You can purchase ready-assembled frames, with the weldwire already attached, or you can make your own. If you decide on the latter course, use 3.8cm(1.5in)-square, or thicker, timber for the frames. This will stand up to most weather conditions. It should be treated with a suitable preservative such as creosote, creosote substitute (USA), or one of the many colored wood paints. The

they could be mounted onto a low wall. The latter is the more pleasing to look at but of course is the more costly option. You could use cinder blocks and clad these with wood, or cement, or you could use house bricks or the more costly natural stone. Whatever your most popular weldwire will be 19G 2.5x1.25cm (1x1/2in) hole size, though 1.25 (1/2in) square would be the ideal. If you live in an area where there are birds of prey, ravens, butcher birds, or snakes, it is wise to double clad the frames. That is, to place weldwire on each side of the frame. This obviously doubles the cost of the weldwire but may prove the less expensive option in the long run.

If you do use single panels of weldwire, place this on the inner edge, as this will make for a more pleasing look to the flight. You will then need to fix wooden or plastic battens over the edges so there is no risk that the budgies will whittle away on any exposed edges, nor get their toes or legbands caught on the pre-cut ends of the weldwire. Weldwire comes in various cut lengths as well as widths — 1-meter widths being the most popular to work with. You can purchase plastic-coated weldwire, but this will push the costs up. You will find that if you paint the weldwire with a bitumen paint, this will not only increase its life, but will also making viewing into the flight much better. You will not notice the weldwire as easily as if it is left in its galvanized state.

The panel size will be one meter wide (3ft), which is about the typical width of many flights. Its height would normally be two meters high, which is ideal if the panels are to be fitted onto a wall of about 30cm(12in). However, two meters would be just a little short if the panels were being fixed from the floor level. What you need to avoid is having the roof cross members distracting

Make sure your budgie's living quarters are roomy enough to accommodate his favorite toy.

your view of the flight, which is what will happen if the total height is under two meters.

Using a panel system to create the flights offers many advantages over stapling the weldwire to a pre-erected framework. Should you wish to expand the aviaries, this is easily achieved by removing one or two panels. In the event that one or more panels should deteriorate more than others, they can be replaced. If you move, you can simply dismantle the panels and assemble them on the new property.

Protection from the elements is a key consideration in selecting a site for your aviary.

This aviary features an elevated shelter area for its occupants.

WEATHER PROTECTION

The amount of weather protection an aviary needs will obviously reflect both the country it is in and the general locale of the site. Such protection can be of a permanent or temporary nature. The roof can be partly or totally covered with plain or tinted corrugated plastic sheeting. This gives protection against rain, snow, and cold winds, yet allows the maximum of light to enter the flight. If you live in a warm country, you might consider using bamboo wattling. This is attractive yet allows the sun to filter through into the flight. An alternative, for both the roof and parts of the aviary sides, would be to have panels of flat plastic that could be screwed into place as needed, depending on the prevailing season.

If only part of the roof is protected, do bear in mind that when rains are heavy you are likely to get a lot of water pouring into the flight. With this in mind, it would be wise to have the corrugated panels facing the outer edge of the flight and slightly raised in the middle, or at one side, so the rain is channeled away from the aviary.

Whilst discussing protection you may wish to include a false roof in the flight so that cats or birds of prey cannot reach the budgerigars. Such a false roof should be about 15cm (6in) or so below the top roof. The alternative is to place some large-hole-size weldwire a few inches above the roof. Cats and birds of prey do not feel secure on this so they tend to ignore the roof after their initial attempts to walk on it.

FLIGHT DECORATION

You can make an aviary flight extremely attractive with just a little thought, and some extra cost. You could add a covered walkway or portal along the front of the aviaries and hang potted plants from this, or maybe a creeping vine. The roof supports to this could be of the rustic pole type. The latter could also be extended from the front of the aviary roof and protrude beyond the walkway. The uprights could be mounted onto a low natural brick wall; the effect is really magnificent.

In a row of aviaries, you might have one higher than

the others
and with a
pitched roof. You could
place raised boarding along
the front of the aviary roof
and fashion an interesting
shape out of this. Conifers
and shrubs planted in tubs
can be situated such that

An aviary should be roomy enough for the hobbyist to perform routine maintenance tasks with ease.

they provide a windbreak
and add a touch of green to
the outside of the aviaries.
Within the flight itself

you could include a fountain. This would be well used by the birds and add a touch of interest. You might include a small rock escarpment for the birds to play on. You could place trays of turf in the flight for the budgerigars to peck over — removing and replacing this as needed. There is no need for the flight to look stark and utilitarian for want of a little imagination.

Perches can either be of the dowel type or, better still, be of natural branches. Do not clutter the flight, but place the perches at each end to provide the maximum flying distance down the length. As for the actual size of the flight, this is obviously controlled by space and costs. The bigger it is the better, and the more scope it gives you to furnish it. Remember, you may want to expand your collection in the future.

THE BIRDROOM

The birdroom can be a room of many uses. It can provide indoor flights for the outside aviaries, can be used as a storeroom for all of your seed and equipment, and can house breeding or stock cages. It can be no more than a shed added to the flights, or it can be a specially built unit that could cost thousands of dollars to erect and equip. Some that I have seen were quite magnificent and equipped with TV monitors, computers, fire and security alarms, and specially built storage units, cages and flights.

If possible, try to hook up electric, water, and sewerage, so life is much easier when attending day-to-day chores. You can purchase birdrooms from specialist suppliers, but some breeders design and build or have built their

All windows in the aviary shelter should be securely covered with wire mesh to prevent escapes and injury caused by the birds' flying into the glass.

own. The main consideration with a birdroom is that it is well lighted, well ventilated, and well insulated.

If you purchase a ready-made unit and you do not have a concrete or slab base to place it on, stand it on a few bricks so there is ample air circulating under the floor boards. This will prolong its life and reduce the risk of rodents burrowing up through the earth and thence into the birdroom. The floor should be covered with an easy-clean linoleum or tiles. The walls will be better for being lined, and with an insulating material placed in the cavity created. Electrical wiring can also be placed in the cavity before the lining is added.

Air vents should be placed both low to the floor and high up to provide the maximum benefit. Windows should be included in the design because birds do not like flying into darkened rooms. They should be

because they allow for some storage room beneath the flight. There should be a pop hole in the indoor flight so birds can fly in and out

Unfortunately, the theft of birds does occur. Take every precaution to burglar-proof your aviary.

covered with weldwire so they can be opened on warm days yet be secure against the possibility of birds escaping should they be loose in the room — also in case the glass should get broken.

Internal flights from the aviaries can be full or half height. The latter are useful if you are tight on space,

from the aviary as they so wish. A landing platform is useful. The pop hole should have a door on it so the birds can be shut in the birdroom during really bad weather, or if you want to catch them. By fitting a rod or other device from this door to the outer edge of the flight you can open and close it without the need to enter the aviary. You may even have a stable-type door to the outer flights so that the birds can more easily fly in and out during nice weather. The feeder dishes should be placed in the birdroom flight to encourage the birds back at night.

Allow yourself plenty of cupboard and food preparation areas. Although many breeders include an isolation area for sick birds and a quarantine area in the birdroom, this is not recommended, for obvious reasons. If possible, site these away from your stock.

It is useful if you can fit a safety porch to the birdroom entrance (and to any outside entrances to the flights). Such a porch is simply a mesh-clad area you enter before entering the birdroom or aviary. Should a bird swoop by you when you open the birdroom door, it will only get into the safety porch, thus not escape. If the porch is fitted with a good padlock, it makes the aviary unit that little bit more secure from potential thieves.

BIRDROOM FITTINGS

Under this heading will come lighting, heating, cooling, and air cleansing equipment. The range of equipment now available to the aviculturist is tremendous when compared with the situation that pertained not so many years ago.

1. Lighting. Fluorescent lights are your best and most economical form of lighting. There is a wide range to choose from; the daylight models are perhaps the best, as they give off a light that almost equates to that of sunlight. It is wise to invest in a dimmer switch so that the light gradually gets

dimmer according to how you have programmed it. This is very useful in the winter months when you are working in the birdroom after dark. The light will slowly go off when you have finished, rather than suddenly if it is switched off. The latter situation always startles the birds, and they may fly into the mesh of their flight, or onto the floor, and remain there until the next morning.

Those living in the USA are fortunate in that they can purchase light-sensitive lights for a very reasonable cost. These are of great value for birdkeepers, because they automatically switch on and off depending on the amount of light hitting them. They are excellent night lights. Similar lights are available in other countries but at a much higher cost. You could, however, simply

have a low-wattage lamp in the birdroom at night so any birds that are startled by car headlights or other disturbances can see their way back to the perches without problem. It is wise to include external night lights near your birdroom door. This will deter thieves and no doubt shed some light onto the aviary flight, so any birds startled into this will be able to find their way back into the shelter.

2. Heating/Cooling. Many breeders do not have a heating facility in their birdrooms because this can result in an overhot situation. However, it does offer benefit to those who breed in the winter months and does make working in the birdroom a little more pleasant at this time, especially if you are elderly. The object is to ensure the temperature does not fall unduly low, nor rise such

This budgie perch features a gravel tray in which the birds can scratch around.

that there is a dramatic difference between the outside and inside temperatures. With this in mind, you should be looking to hold the upper limit at about 55°F(13°C) and the lower at around 46°F(8°C).

There are many heaters available to choose from, but the best are probably tubular electric or oil-filled electric. These can be purchased with thermostats built into them. Fan heaters are less desirable because they tend to blow dust about. On no account should you use kerosene (paraffin) heaters because you cannot control their temperature and they may give off harmful fumes. Some breeders in the UK will have water-generated domestic central heating supplied to their birdrooms, whilst in the USA the choice might be forced air propane, though you would need a large birdroom to invest to this sort of level.

A means of cooling the birdroom is beneficial in very hot climates both to reduce the risk of bacterial and parasitic growth and also so the birds are not discouraged from breeding because it is too hot. Extractor fans mounted high up in the birdroom will help keep the temperature down somewhat, as will ceiling-mounted fans. However, they will also kick up the dust, so be real sure you keep on top of cleaning.

Evaporator coolers can be useful, providing they are wired through a thermostat that regulates the lower temperature — otherwise the birds will soon become chilled even though it is really hot outside! You might also use a standard fan, and if this is directed over a bucket of water it will also increase the humidity if this is needed. You could, of course, purchase a humidifier if dry air is a problem in your area, or a dehumidifier if the reverse was the case.

3. Air Cleanliness. In order to overcome the problem of bacteria and dust in the birdroom, the ionizer is the answer. These are now very popular and come in a range of models from the inexpensive to the very costly. They emit millions of negative ions and these collide with dust and bacteria, killing the

latter and making the former much heavier. Dust thus falls to the floor or onto surfaces where it is easily wiped away. Ionizers will also neutralize tobacco smells if you are a smoker. The ionizer is wired into your electric supply, or simply inserted into a convenient socket — even a lamp holder. It should be left on 24 hours a day and the cost of so doing really is minimal. You may need more than one unit depending on the area to be covered. Some can be run from a car battery: check this out when you look into their purchase. Most avicultural suppliers will stock a range of models.

Feeding utensils should be sturdy and non-tippable. Pet shops stock a variety of such items.

FEEDING UTENSILS

Whether you have a number of birds in a communal aviary, or pairs in a cage or small flight, there are seed and water feeders galore to choose from. For pairs, the standard tubular or oblong automatic dispensers will be fine. If a number of birds are using the feeder, then the inverted glass jar feeders are useful. The jar is placed onto a base with a raised edge so seed can fall by gravity into the base. As the birds eat, more seed falls down. You can also purchase round chicken type feeders for both seed and water. Always be aware that seed dispensers can clog. By tapping the dispenser each day you can check if it is releasing the seed as it should.

Always check that water dispensers are not frozen during bad weather. If you have a large run of aviaries or cages, you can fit an automatic watering unit. Some breeders prefer to feed their birds in open dishes, which are placed on the floor of the internal flight or under a covered part of the aviary. Flat aluminum dog bowls can also be used.

Nutrition

Budgerigars are extremely easy birds to cater for in terms of their nutrition. If you have only one or two pet birds, it is not essential that you under-stand the technicalities of feeding, because you can purchase ready-mixed seeds for budgerigars. These have been specially blended: extra vitamins and minerals have been added to them in order to create a livable diet. However, you may wish to understand more about nutrition so you are more in tune with the needs of your pets.

Breeders should certainly have a reasonably sound basic understanding of the dietary needs of their birds because they will find it more economical to prepare their own seed mixtures. Further, many failures in the

If you have a number of budgies, it is economical to buy seed in bulk quantities. If you have only one bird, however, this is not practical as seed has a limited storage life.

breeding room are directly attributable to an inadequate diet. The same is true of problems such as cannibalism and egg mortality. In pet birds, the habit of feather plucking may be created by a lack of something in the diet.

BASIC REQUIREMENTS

The budgerigar is a seed-eating bird, as are most parrots. The usual budgie mix will comprise millet and canary seed with other seeds added in small amounts. Whilst this mix will enable your budgerigar to survive, it hardly constitutes a well-balanced diet, for it is short of many essential ingredients.

Fed on such a regimen your birds may well live for many years, though this fact should not be construed to mean it is proof of being sufficient. As the famous aviculturist the Duke of Bedford is purported to have said to a lady when confronted with a parrot that had been fed purely on a basic seed ration, 'Madam, your bird is not living, it is merely taking a long while to die!' This, I think, places seed-only diets in a good perspective.

It must always be remembered that in its wild habitat the budgerigar would consume a wide ranging diet that embraced greenfoods, fruits, and a certain amount of animal protein in the form of invertebrates. Further, the seeds eaten are often unripe, and of course always fresh. The fact that budgerigars were found to be able to exist on an all-seed diet when they were originally imported into Europe in the 19th century has tended to shape attitudes with regards to most parrot species. The more nutrition is studied in

The basic element of the budgerigar's diet consists of a variety of seeds. The millet spray shown here can easily be clipped onto your pet's cage.

Regular supplements of greenfoods are recommended for a nutritionally balanced budgie diet.

relation to parrotlike birds, the more it is realized that the diet must be very varied — even if some of that variety is offered only in small amounts.

EATING HABITS

Birds are creatures of habit — aren't we all — and that which they are not familiar with is invariably rejected. This fact accounts for the reason many breeders will state that when offered variety their birds refused it. Only when problems arise do they then experiment in a more diligent manner by devising ways to encourage their stock to try foods previously rejected. It is a chicken and egg situation. The adults have been fed only on seeds, with maybe a few greenfoods. The chicks eat only what they are fed by their parents and what they see others eat. In turn, they will bring their own chicks up in the same manner.

Just like people, budgerigars have different preferences when it comes to food. A picky budgie can be coaxed to eat by your offering it a varied diet.

Somehow, the circle must be penetrated so the birds will take a varied diet, which they will in turn encourage, by example, their chicks to take.

THE ROLE OF DIFFERING FOODS

To understand the importance of various foods, it is useful to look at the basic constituents of them and see how they are used in the body. This may shed light on the values of differing foods and their importance in a well-balanced diet.

1. Carbohydrates. Seeds such as canary and millet are rich in carbohydrates. These latter compounds are broadly described as sugars in various forms. Some are simple, others are complex. They comprise carbon, hydrogen, and oxygen. Other than seeds, all cereal crops, such as rice, maize, and wheat, as well as their byproducts (bread, cookies, breakfast cereals) are rich in carbohydrates. Their main role is to provide energy, with water and carbon dioxide being byproducts of their oxidization in the body. Carbohydrates provide food with bulk, and they also determine which bacteria will live in the digestive tract. They perform numerous other functions in the body, such as enabling fat to be used efficiently.

2. Fats. These substances are the most concentrated form of energy, yielding twice that of carbohydrates or proteins. They make food palatable and many are rich sources of vitamins, such as A, D, E, and K. They perform many other roles in the body and are found in seeds, animal, and vegetable oils, and in association with meat and dairy products.

They can be stored in the tissues and serve as a layer of insulation, as well as a buffer to protect internal organs from undue damage during muscular activity and general day-to-day life. They represent a ready means of energy in the event that the carbohydrate levels fall below that needed to satisfy muscular needs.

3. Proteins. These compounds are the building blocks of tissue. The skin, the eyes, the blood, the brain, and even the genes of animals are essentially made up of protein. They are composed of what are called amino acids. Some of the latter can be synthesized in the bird's body, others cannot and must be supplied via the food. Not all the essential amino acids are found in foods of vegetable origin. Like fats, proteins can be oxidized to yield carbohydrates when normal foods are scarce, which is why any animal gets thinner when it has no food. The body tissues are broken down to provide the energy for muscular needs. Fecal matter is largely the residue of proteins after they have passed through the digestive system; its odor is the volatile degradation of

Water bottles and feeders that can be filled from the outside of the cage are convenient and time-saving. Additionally, their design can help to prevent the birds' contaminating their water and food with their droppings.

proteins. Protein-rich foods include meat, butter and other dairy products, eggs, fish, and many seeds.

4. Vitamins. These compounds are not really foods but without them life would not be possible. They are essential to all cellular activity and formation. Certain vitamins can be synthesized in birds (via the feathers or in the digestive tract), others cannot. If any

are missing, the result will be ill health in one form or another. Conversely, if in excess, they can inhibit the function of others, so a careful balance is needed with them. Vitamin-rich foods include fruits, oils, meats, and certain vegetables.

5. Minerals. These substances include iron, calcium, iodine, sulfur, magnesium, potassium, phosphorous, sodium, copper, and many others. Some of them, such as calcium and phosphorous, are crucial to bone structure, whereas with others their importance has not actually been determined. All foods contain minerals, and, of course, materials such as grit, concrete, eggshells, and many other substances are made up of minerals.

6. Unidentified Factors. There are still many unidentified substances in food. Their importance may be almost nil or vital to the well-being of animals, depending on the substance. That they exist is demonstrated by feeding laboratory animals with all known pure ingredients and comparing the growth, reproduction rate, and so on with others that are fed on natural foods. Any improvement is the result of the unknown factors. All vitamins were once unknown factors, so it is impossible to say what vital ingredients of food remain to be identified — or in what foods they exist.

7. Water. No living organism can survive without water. Although this compound is a byproduct of body metabolism, this cannot meet the needs of birds or other animals. They must drink — to a greater or lesser degree. If they

The cage tray must be cleaned on a regular basis. Maintaining sanitary conditions for your budgie is an important part of good animal husbandry.

consume fruits, they will drink less than if they do not, because fruits are largely water in content, as are greenfoods. Water is also very variable in its content. Some contains more minerals than others. Faucet (tap) water is chlorinated to make it drinkable. Once water has been standing for any length of time, it rapidly deteriorates as more and more bacteria colonize it. Eventually, it can be almost like poison, so you should never assume that water is water and that as long as a bird has some it will be suitable to drink because it originally came from the faucet.

THE QUALITY OF SEEDS

We all know that some foods are better than others, even within the same sorts. If we apply this logic to seeds, it will be appreciated that these, too, can be very variable, depending on many factors. For example, the longer we keep a food we know it will steadily deteriorate — seeds are no different. When seed is purchased there is no way of knowing when it was harvested: this year, last year, or two years ago? Was it stored under good conditions, or was it kept in a damp place, or exposed to bright sunlight before it was shipped to its destination? How long has the grower had it before selling it to a pet store, and how has the latter looked after it? Clearly, some seeds could be almost worthless in terms of their nutritional content by the time you or I purchase it. Likewise, seed is grown in many parts of the world, some in nutrient-rich soils, some in poor soil. The soil will determine the value of the seeds' contents, as will the time of the year it is harvested. When all of these factors are taken into account, the only conclusion that can be drawn is that, like water, there are seeds and there are seeds. If a bird is fed purely on a restricted selection of seeds, it follows that this leaves a great deal to chance as to whether those seeds are supplying the needed nutritional content. With an apple you can see if it is good or bad, but this is far more difficult when it comes to seeds.

Quite naturally, we all

The seed that you feed your budgie should always be the freshest. To help maintain the seed's freshness, it should be stored in an area that is free of dampness.

assume the seed we feed to our birds is basically of good content, but it would seem wise to both feed as much seed variety as we can, as well as supply other foods to ensure, one way or the other, nothing is deficient in terms of ingredients. Further, it is evident that seeds alone cannot supply certain vital ingredients that can only come from animal origins. When a wild budgerigar eats seeds it will eat anything clinging to that seed — such as insects. Small though they may be, they will, on a collective basis, add up to a meaning-ful supply of protein. Grubs in fruit, as well as samplings of the fruit, will meet protein and vitamin needs of the wild birds.

We cannot really know all

Today's budgie hobbyist can choose from a wide variety of foods that are specially formulated for the good nutritional health of his birds.

of the foods wild budgerigars eat, nor can we supply many of those we do know about because they are not available to us. We can, however, supply their equivalents, and other foods that contain known important constituents.

ENCOURAGING GOOD FEEDING HABITS

If a budgerigar will not accept the range of foods we know are good for it, how do we persuade it to sample them? This can be done in numerous ways.

1. Withdrawal. If you place an unknown food, be it a seed or fruit or whatever, in front of your bird when it has its regular seeds available, it will obviously ignore the strange food. It may sample it but often will then leave it. If, however, you remove its

regular food for a short while, it may just be hungry enough to try the new one. I hasten to add you must not withhold food for too long, just long enough — maybe 2 to 3 hours — to encourage the bird to try the new one. If it does not then supply its regular seed.

2. Impregnation. Let us say your bird will not eat apple. Cut up a small piece and push some of its favorite seeds into this. Remove the seed pot. This may prompt the bird to take the seed from the apple — and it will also take a little apple with this. It may just

A good diet will be reflected in the overall appearance of your budgerigar.

find it likes it. You can do this with any other fruits you might wish to offer to your bird.

3. Other Birds. If you have one or two birds that already take a varied menu, place them with stock that does not, or with youngsters. The latter two groups may be tempted to test the new food. Birds are influenced greatly by what they see conspecifics eating.

4. Strategic Placement. If a new food is placed on the floor, a bird may ignore it. Place the same food in a strategic spot, such as next to its perch, and it may well nibble at it off and on. Eventually it may decide it likes the new food. You can also hang it from a branch in an aviary so it becomes a plaything that gets nibbled.

5. Change its Presentation. If a bird rejects a given dry seed, it may well take it willingly if it has been soaked in water for 24 hours. Or it may enjoy it in the sprouted form. From this point it may then accept the dry seed. A vegetable refused on its own may be taken if mixed with something that is liked. Seed can be soaked in various extracts of a food and then allowed to dry.

6. Work on the Chicks. Chicks are far less fussy in their eating habits than adults. At this age they really do not know what they are supposed to eat and this comes via 'instruction' from the parents. You can offer them tiny pieces of various foods whilst they are still in the nest or shortly after they leave it. If they can be encouraged to take a wide variety, they will supply this to their own chicks if it is maintained as part of the normal diet.

7. Seasonal. A bird may refuse a food at one time of

the year yet be more than willing to take it at another — especially during the breeding season.

You can see that there are a number of ways of trying your bird with a range of foods. The more you can encourage it to try, the more willing it becomes to try other foods. All too often owners quit too early and fall back on old ideas — budgies don't need this or that. This is a convenient outlet for not persevering.

SUPPLEMENTS

Under this heading can be included vitamin

The white object clipped to the side of this budgie's cage is a cuttlebone, which is an excellent source of calcium. All budgies should be offered this supplement.

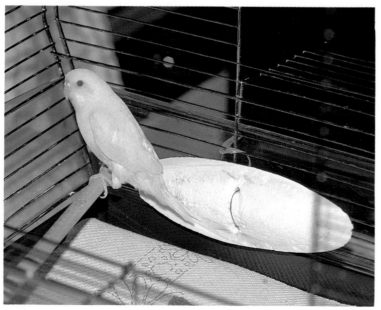

supplements, iodine blocks, salt, and grit. Taking them in order, it has already been pointed out that an excess of vitamins can be dangerous. For example too much vitamin A will destroy vitamin E and may be a contributory cause of French molt. The ratio of one vitamin to another may be deleterious to birds in some supplements. When needed, supplements can be extremely beneficial, but how are you to know when this is so? It has become somewhat the 'in thing' to use supplements these days, but unless the diet is lacking, such use is rarely needed and then only after veterinary advice. When antibiotics have been used, supplements may be required because these drugs may kill beneficial bacteria in the digestive tract, and which synthesize certain vitamins.

Apart from good nutrition, your budgie must be given ample opportunity for undisturbed sleep. Too little sleep can make your pet nervous and tense. Many budgie keepers cover their birds' cages at bedtime.

Iodine has been shown to be of some importance to budgerigars. If it is lacking,

(blocks), I am not sure of the basis behind its value but was told many years ago of its usefulness in preventing feather plucking. I have never suffered with feather pluckers, and have given small amounts of salt in a dish — whether this is of value, or whether the wide-ranging diet I give is the reason for having no problems I would not like to say.

Birds have no teeth and so have only a limited means, via the beak, of crushing food. However, they swallow small pieces of grit when pecking around on the floor. This mixes with the seeds, and in the gizzard the strong muscles, together with the grit, churn the seeds into a pasty mulch that can then be more easily acted upon by digestive juices. The grit size should be suited to budgies; if it is too small it will be less

it may increase the risk of goiter, a thyroid disease, as well as result in stunted growth and other side effects. Young breeding stock may be especially at risk, so an iodine block is recommended in cages and aviaries. With regards to salt

A budgerigar needs grit, or gravel, to help it grind up the food in its crop. Grit should be available to your budgie at all times.

effective. Your pet shop will have a suitable size. Other sources of grit are garden soil, eggshells, and oystershell.

MIXED OR SEPARATE SEED?

The question of how to present the seeds to your birds will depend on numerous factors. If you have only one or two pet budgerigars, then it is probably just as well to purchase ready-mixed seeds in packets. The quality of these is normally extremely high. There will be some wastage, as the birds throw out those seeds they do not like at all — but the cost of this will be minimal. The breeder, with many birds to feed, will find it more advantageous to supply at least certain of the seeds in their own container, probably the millet and the canary seed. Other seeds can be mixed in a third container. Even these could initially be given in separate dishes in order to establish a ratio of one to another in those eaten. A mix can then be made based on this. Time is always a factor for the breeder, and this often prompts them to simply mix all the seeds together, but it really is worthwhile finding out what ratio your birds like of one to the other. This differs from one breeder to another depending on the source (country) and quality of the seeds they purchase. If you purchase a winnowing machine, this will cut down the loss of seeds that are mixed and are discarded by the birds.

Birds that are finicky eaters are likely to suffer nutritional deficiencies. Fortunately, vitamin and mineral supplements are available that can remedy this problem.

SOME POPULAR SEEDS

The list of seeds that can be fed to your budgerigars is very extensive, but normally

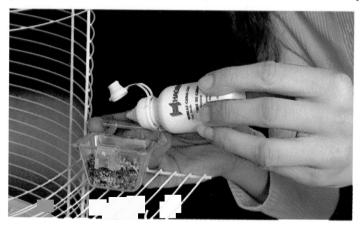

The numerous budgie products on the market today help to make the keeping of these birds relatively carefree.

the following are the ones most used and readily available. Some are acquired tastes and some are considerably more expensive than others. You will also find that breeders vary considerably in their choice of which seeds they feel are best for these birds. The only way you will know for sure is to try them yourself. If you discarded every seed and food item you heard was of no value to your birds, then you would probably end up feeding them canary and millet, with little else offered!

The nutrient values given are approximates, as these will vary for the reasons already discussed.

1. Millet. This comes in various forms, such as panicum, white, yellow, red, and Japanese. It is also available 'on the ear' in the form of sprays, the French variety being rather more

costly than that from China. Panicum is a small round variety that is usually included in most mixes. Red and Japanese are rarely given to budgies. Millets are high in carbohydrates (about 66%) and low in proteins (10-12%) and fats (4%), so are prime energy seeds. Millet sprays are much relished, but do not feed them in excess. You can soak them for 24 hours (and any seeds) and these will be greatly appreciated. The panicum part of the basic diet is normally 40-60%.

2. Canary Seed. This elongate seed is usually imported from various countries — Canada, Australia, Morocco, and Spain being popular sources. Prices vary depending on the source (Moroccan being the more costly in recent years). Canary seed has a slightly lower carbohydrate value

Millet spray, shown here, is greatly relished by budgies, but never feed it to the exclusion of other basic seed foods.

(58%) and higher protein (14%) and fat (6%) than panicum and is just slightly more expensive. The basic diet will comprise about the same ratio as panicum.

3. Niger. This small black seed is low in carbohydrate (15%) and rich in protein (17%) and especially in fats (32%). It is very expensive when compared to the basic seeds discussed, but is an important seed that should be included in any mix. As with any oil (fat)-rich seed, you must watch for any that have damaged or split shells. This will make the oil rancid and such seeds are very dangerous to your birds.

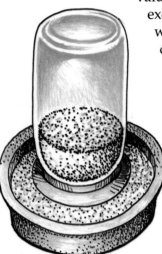

Illustration of a gravity-activated feeder. This type of feeder is especially useful if you are going to leave your budgie alone for the better part of the day.

4. Hemp. This was once an inexpensive seed, but its cost has risen greatly over the years, though it is still much cheaper than niger. Some breeders are suspicious of its value, but it is an excellent seed with values corresponding to those of niger. It is a round seed, brown in color. Add to the mix in moderation.

5. Sunflower. This seed is seen in three varieties (white, black, and striped) and is often in large or small sizes, the latter being most suited to budgerigars. Its values are carbohydrate (21%), protein (20%) and

Millet is high in carbo-hydrates and thus is a good "energy food" for budgies. Some budgies like their millet completely dry; others prefer it to be soaked.

fats (30%). The black varieties are often ignored by birds whilst the white is often the favored choice. Amongst the many other potential seeds often offered by seed merchants are the following. Maw and rape: two seeds that are very rich in fats (40%). Safflower: rather like sunflower in appearance, but is quite a bit cheaper. Linseed (flax): good protein content (21%) and fat rich (35%). Its carbohydrate value is around 25%; a good general seed with a cost comparable to hemp, maybe a little cheaper. Oats and groats (dehusked oats), maize, and wheat: cereal seeds that are rich in carbohydrates and low in fats. They are not commonly fed to budgies but may be enjoyed when soaked.

Teazle, gold of pleasure, and lettuce are unusual seeds but all worth trying, though they are very expensive. Many nuts are enjoyed by budgerigars if they are crushed into suitably small pieces. The seeds of all wild grasses will be taken, with few rejections. You can see that the list of seeds could go on and on, it being a case that certain ones have become traditional, available, and therefore very convenient for the feeding of most cage and aviary birds. By all means experiment because you can only gain by so doing.

SOAKING AND SPROUTING

For young, breeding or ailing birds, soaked and sprouted seeds offer numerous advantages. The seed shell is weakened, making it easier for the bird to break this. It also commences the germination process and increases the protein and vitamin levels. This affects the taste of the seed and seems to appeal to most birds. To soak the seeds, place them in a flat, small container. Immerse them in warm water, cover the top, and place in a darkened cupboard for 24 hours. They are then given a thorough rinse in cold water and fed to the birds early in the day, or in the late

Top left: Preparing seed for germination. **Top right, center, and bottom:** Growing grass from seed. Sprinkle seed over earth and then mix together. Spray lightly with water and store in a warm, dark place.

afternoon as the case may be. Any that are not eaten within 12 hours are best removed; otherwise, they are likely to be attacked by mold or bacteria. To sprout the seeds repeat the soaking stage but after rinsing them place them on a tray of blotting or similar paper and return them to the darkened cupboard for 24-36 hours. By this time small shoots will be visible. Rinse again and feed to the birds. Any that fail to germinate indicates a seed of low quality. This is a useful test for seed quality. You can soak or sprout most seeds. Many breeders will sprout grass, cress, spinach, canary seed, and other plants, which are then left in the trays for the birds to peck over. In this way you can grow a supply of fresh foods all the year round, as long as you have a suitably warm room or greenhouse for sprouting plants during the winter.

GREENFOODS AND FRUITS

Greenfoods in their many forms, together with fruits, provide most of the vitamin needs of your budgerigars. You will find that some breeders do not recommend the use of too many greenfoods during the breeding season because they tend to make the fecal matter more liquid, thus the nest dirtier. Actually, this is the very time that breeding birds do need a wide variety of foods, especially those rich in vitamins. Obviously, if they are fed in excess, this may create problems, but in moderation there should be no cause for alarm.

One of the problems with greenfoods is that some breeders will suddenly start supplying them in the spring, when many wild

plants become available, and it is this that creates the difficulties. No food item should ever be supplied suddenly and in quantity; this is asking for trouble. If your birds are accustomed to eating greenfoods and fruit, then these will not unduly change the state of their fecal matter. To withhold such foods during the breeding season has no

Never place your budgie's cage near plants that are poisonous, such as poinsettia. A budgie is curious and will frequently nibble at anything within reach of its beak, sometimes with tragic results.

merit at all.

The most popular wild plants used in aviculture are dandelion (*Taraxacum* spp), chickweed (*Stellaria* spp), meadow and other grasses (*Poa* spp), shepherd's purse

(*Capsella* spp), sow thistle (*Sonchus* spp), and plantain (*Plantago* spp). You can give the birds the entire plant — hanging it up at a convenient location. Replace it each day, by which time the birds will have lost interest in it as it dries. Before supplying any greenfoods, especially wild plants, they must be rinsed in water. If not, there is the danger that any residual insecticides used by farmers may be on them. Do not gather from verges that may have been contaminated by exhaust fumes or dogs. You could, of course, cultivate wild plants in your garden — or in the greenhouse during the winter months.

You can offer your birds a range of vegetables and fruits and some will be eaten, others ignored. Birds are just like us in that their preferences vary from one individual to another. Chop up the foods to form a small dish of salad and offer fresh each day (morning or late afternoon so they escape the peak heat of the sun). By mixing in some favored supplemental seed you will encourage the birds to try the salad. All fruits and vegetables are, of course, essentially made up of water, but it is the vitamin and element content that is important. Never feed any plants that are grown from a bulb, as these are poisonous.

Cod liver oil is a rich source of vitamins and a few drops can be poured over a seed mix — not too much though. It cannot be left too long otherwise it will turn rancid, so only supply it sparingly and discard uneaten seeds after a few hours.

PROTEIN FOODS

All breeding birds should be given protein-rich foods.

Greenfoods should be fed to your budgie in small quantity only. To avoid upsetting your pet's digestion, make sure that any greenfood that is offered is as fresh as that which you yourself would consume.

Indeed, any budgerigars will benefit from these, as they will supply all the essential amino acids needed by your birds in order to build sound tissue. You can obtain high-protein foods from your pet store, or you can prepare mashes from items found in your kitchen. Amongst the latter are skimmed milk, buttermilk, butter, lard, egg yolk, cheese, beef extracts, honey, wheat germ oil, and finely minced meats. These can be mixed with crushed oats, bread, or cookie crumble to form a mash that is just damp. Again, some seeds can be added to the concoction for birds not accustomed to this type of food.

Many houseplants, beautiful though they may be, are poisonous. If you are unsure about the classification (poisonous or non-poisonous) of any of your house-plants, keep your budgie away from them.

Do not mix too much, otherwise it will be wasted. You can keep it for a few days in the refrigerator and use it as needed. Be sure it has time to thaw out. If milk is included, the life of the mash will be short because it will quickly sour on warm days — so feed early in the morning. If honey is used, this might attract wasps. On this account many birdkeepers do not use it, so try it and see how you go. You may find that your budgerigars enjoy certain livefoods, such as maggots and other larvae of insects. These are available from pet shops. Do not use those that have been color dyed for anglers. Maggots must be cleansed so that the black line (fecal matter) seen running down their back has vanished — this is dangerous to your birds. Place them in sawdust until they are clean and feed a few according to taste during the breeding season. Livefoods are not essential if you are already supplying a protein supplement or mash.

Note the handy device that holds this budgie's greenfood. Pet shops sell numerous items such as these.

You will find that if you can encourage your budgerigars to accept more than just seed diet, this will show itself in improved health, feather quality, and a dramatic reduction in breeding problems. The chicks will be stronger and

Allowing your pet unlimited access to fruit can cause digestive upset.

themselves more willing to accept a wide ranging diet. If you have a large stud of budgerigars, it is obviously less convenient to feed a wide variety of foods because it involves much more work. I think the effort justifies the time; I would rather keep fewer birds that I can devote time to than many at the expense of their well-being.

OBESITY

Sometimes budgerigars may become obese, usually pet birds and those in birdrooms that have limited aviary access. Should this condition be seen, do not on any account starve the birds as this will result in a deficiency of vitamin production in their metabolism. The answer is to either reduce their rations, ensure they have more time out of their cage or, ideally, both. By reducing their rations, rather than removing certain seeds, you do not risk denying them the benefits of a well-rounded diet.

Stock Selection

The ways in which you will go about the business of selecting one or more budgerigars will be governed by the reason you want the budgerigar in the first place. It may be as a pet, as an exhibition bird, for breeding, or purely as an aviary bird in a mixed collection. Each of these will be discussed, but whatever the reason for wanting budgerigars the first consideration must be in the selection of healthy birds.

THE HEALTHY BUDGERIGAR

In assessing the health of a budgie, your first judgment should be in relation to the premises and conditions under which the bird is being kept. These will tell you much about the potential health of the stock on view. If the premises look untidy and in need of a good clean, then things are not promising — I would immediately look elsewhere. The cages in which the birds are kept should look clean. The perches should display no signs of hardened fecal matter, and any accumulation of this on the cage floor, under the perches, is not good. Cages should not be overcrowded such that the birds are forced to pack together on the perches. The food and water containers should be clean and well supplied.

Seed should be in containers with lids and not open to being covered in dust and debris. The room in which the birds are housed should be warm, not overpoweringly hot. It should be well ventilated. If the stock is in an aviary, this

Budgerigars come in a lovely array of colors and patterns—
something for everyone!

should have a floor that can easily be hosed down. There should be no piles of vegetation near the aviary — such as clippings, leaves, or other garden trimmings. These are potential breeding grounds for pathogens. If all looks well, then you can proceed to the next stage: viewing the birds.

Do not get too close to the cages or aviary initially. Stand back a few feet and let the birds settle down. In this way any that are not feeling so well will not be startled into flight by your presence. Any budgies that remain on their perch uninterested when others around are very active, are invariably not in the best of health. A bird that is asleep will have its head turned through ninety degrees so its beak rests at the base of its neck. Its feathers will be fluffed up and it will perch on one leg.

If it has its head dropped so its beak is in its chest, its head feathers are fluffed and both feet are on the perch, this is not a good sign, the more so if it has perched away from the rest of the birds. If no such birds are seen then you can attend the final stage, which is the inspection of the birds. Commence with the head. The eyes should be clear, any signs of cloudiness or weeping or swelling would indicate an illness. They will open fully and not partly. They are round and sparkling.

The cere, the fleshy skin around the nostrils, will not be swollen or uneven on one side compared to the other. There will be no nasal discharge, nor any wheezing sound that might

Facing page: A display cage such as this is ideal if you are keeping a number of budgies. Notice that the top allows for plenty of light.

suggest the bird is having difficulty in breathing. The beak must be well formed. In parrots the upper mandible should fit neatly over that of the lower mandible and should not be unduly long. If the lower mandible protrudes in front of the upper one, this is known as being undershot and is a bad fault that you certainly do not want in any bird you purchase. It may be of genetic origin or due to poor management when the bird was a chick.

The beak itself will be quite smooth in a young bird but less so in an adult if viewed under a hand lens. On no account will it display flaky encrustations or tiny holes in a honey-comb fashion. This could indicate scaly face. This condition is easily cured but should not be there in the first place — it is a sign of minuscule mites. There should be no evidence that the feathers of the head are missing or flaked and powdery.

The feet of a budgerigar should have two toes facing forward and two backwards. This arrangement is called zygodactyl. The nails should be complete with none missing. If a nail is missing, this will make it more difficult for the bird to perch correctly. In turn this will make reproduction more difficult because the bird may not be able to grasp the perch well enough during mating. Further, a missing nail means that the bird must compensate by shifting its weight distribution to another part of the toe and leg. This can lead to deformity. None of these facts may affect the bird's general well being, especially from the viewpoint of a pet bird, but

The health of your prospective budgie is more important than the bird's color and markings.

physical flaws are not desirable — such birds are best left for someone else!

The scales on a bird's legs are evidence of its reptilian ancestry and should lie close to the skin. If they stick outwards this would indicate scaly leg, which is caused by the same mites that create scaly face. Other parasites might also create this situation and, again, whilst this can be overcome there is really no need for you to start off with a problem. Bypass these birds because the chances are that others in the cage or aviary will likewise be infected.

The feathers of a budgerigar should be sleek and none should be obviously missing. Tail feathers may be missing on occasions that may not indicate anything sinister — but it could indicate French molt. Inspect the wing feathers carefully to see if any of their shafts appear brittle or pitted. These could again indicate French molt or feather mite. There is no cure for French molt and thus such birds are of no use to you even though the condition is rarely fatal and the birds appear none the worse for it.

Turn the bird onto its back and inspect the cloacal region. This should be clean and not stained or clogged with dried fecal matter, which would suggest an internal problem, recent or present. Finally, feel the area either side of the breastbone to see that it is well muscled. If the breastbone is evident and there are shallows on either side of it, this is termed going light and indicates a nutritional deficiency.

If the bird has passed your inspection, then you should inspect one or two more of the stock just to satisfy yourself that these are in sound health. This being so you can now turn your attention to the age, color or quality of the bird, depending on your needs.

THE AVIARY BIRD

If one or more budgerigars are required to be added to a mixed aviary collection, the following aspects should be considered. Assuming you live in a temperate weather region, it is best to obtain these birds in the spring, the more so if they are being purchased from a pet store. This is because you will be unaware, unless the dealer knows for sure, whether they have ever lived in an outdoor aviary. Even if they have, they may need to be acclimatized back from the heated store conditions to that of an aviary, and this is best done in the spring.

The quality of the birds

This budgie radiates good health: it is bright-eyed and alert and its plumage is smooth·and even throughout.

may not be important to you if you do not plan especially to breed from them. Generally, where mixed aviaries are concerned, you should not include too many budgerigars, as they might intimidate the other aviary occupants. Cocks are the better choice because if any of the other aviary birds go to nest, hen budgies might just decide to take over the nest, thus killing the chicks or breaking the eggs of the rightful owner.

Budgerigars will coexist quite peacefully with many other species, including the larger finches, some softbills, and other parrots, such as cockatiels and small Australian grass parakeets. Do, however, understand that at breeding times many otherwise peaceful birds can become very aggressive. With this in mind, it is best to build up mixed aviary collections very carefully so you can see how each additional bird mixes in with the community already established.

Budgies for mixed aviaries can be obtained from your local pet shop.

BREEDING STOCK
One source for breeding stock is a breeder, preferably one that is a specialist in the color you are interested in. When looking for breeding stock, you can either watch for someone who is disposing of an entire collection, for one reason or another, or you can purchase individual birds or pairs. The former is usually the more economic proposition and you have less to worry about in terms of quarantining the birds.

Facing page: A budgie in good condition will have a smooth beak, free of any encrustations. The cere, which is the fleshy area around the nostrils, should not be swollen.

However, you will almost certainly have to take all of the birds, including some that are past their best breeding age or are of less than the desired quality you may wish to commence with. If a large stud is up for sale, this would not be a wise choice for a rank beginner, as tempting as it may be. The novice breeder should proceed with just a few pairs and gain experience before trying to maintain many birds. Furthermore, you may find you get disillusioned with breeding, or find that the original stock wasn't so good after all, so must be replaced.

Always purchase the best birds you can afford. Quality, not quantity, is the need of a breeder. Do not be swayed by the fact that you are offered some top-winning birds. These may prove useless for breeding. You need birds that come from a line of sound budgerigars that have a proven record of producing sound birds — and this means healthy birds as well.

It is not important that you have very young birds; indeed, it is better that they have fully molted, which means you can consider any birds that are 1 to 4 years old. This is a good age for your initial stock. You can choose either unproven birds or those that have been bred already. The latter will normally be slightly more expensive because with the former you are talking potential rather than proven breeding ability. You will want birds that carry closed rings (bands) on their legs because this is the only way that a budgerigar's age can be

Facing page: Budgies are not terribly expensive, so why not buy a top-quality specimen?

determined for sure.

A good breeder will have detailed records on the history of his or her stock and you should study these. They should show how many eggs were laid by the various birds bred from, how many were hatched, and how many survived. They will indicate the colors of birds paired and the colors of the offspring. Notes will indicate whether or not the parents were good or bad and give other incidental information. The more data the breeder has on his stock the more likely he is to know its genetic state in relation to colors.

This aspect is very important, especially if you wish to specialize in given colors, and this is recommended. It is always better to concentrate your efforts on just a few colors than on many. Your chances of achieving success will be greater, because you will obviously develop more experience on these rather than if you are trying to spread your efforts too wide — the more so as you will only be starting with a limited number of birds.

There is little merit in obtaining a number of birds from too many sources. The best thing to do is to try and purchase from one, or at most two, sources. This way you are breeding from birds of similar gene lines (assuming the breeder has been established long enough, and knows enough, to have achieved this state). If you draw from two lines, keep these separate until you have developed them long enough to be confident about crossing a bird from one to the other. If you need extra stock in one line, then go back to the breeder who supplied the original birds.

Given this fact, you will

local bird shows and become familiar with who's who in your region. The more background research you place into your initial supplier, the greater your chances of success. Put another way, the less chance

appreciate that you must place much faith in the original breeder, so it is best that such a person lives within a reasonable distance of your own home. If so, maybe he or she can visit your aviaries and offer you sound advice from time to time. This will be less forthcoming if you are buying birds from all over the place.

The best way to locate such a breeder is to visit

This is the correct way to hold your budgie. The first time you try it, your budgie may "protest," but he will eventually get used to the idea.

you will obtain poor stock. The last question you

If you want your pet budgie to become a hand-tame companion, you should select a young bird.

or four cocks and maybe six to eight hens. A few more, or a few less, will be just fine depending on your circumstances. You could even commence with just two pairs or a trio — one cock and two hens. However, there is the possibility that if you have only a few birds they may not 'go to nest'. This is because budgerigars are very social birds and when breeding require the stimulus of others in order to commence breeding activities. The main point is that you never attempt, initially, to overstretch yourself. It is usually easier to expand than it is to cut back, or be swamped with problems too early in your development. Remember, you may not be satisfied with your initial stock or your first aviaries, but you will be stuck with them if you have proceeded too quickly.

may be wondering about in relation to breeding stock is that of how many birds should be obtained. This will obviously depend on a number of factors. How much cash do you have? How much space do you have for aviaries and a birdroom? How much time do you have to devote to your breeding program? Few people have unlimited funds, space, and time. Given the earlier comments of a low key start, a good starting base might be three

EXHIBITION STOCK

The comments made in purchasing breeding birds will clearly apply if you are looking for exhibition birds. There is, however, a fundamental difference. A good breeding bird may not be up to exhibition standards. If you want exhibition-standard breeding birds, these will be the most expensive of all budgerigars. In these you need to combine both proven breeding ability and good looks. Whilst it is theoretically possible for a beginner to purchase sound breeding stock by applying common sense with study of records and seeing a breeder's establishment, this is not so with exhibition stock.

A budgie that is not of exhibition quality can still make a charming and affectionate pet.

If you read the standard of excellence for the show budgerigar, you will find that many birds appear to be of this standard. Only a trained eye can spot all the differences; for these birds you must have a knowledgeable person with you, or go to a well established breeder exhibitor in the first place. If you are honest with the breeder, he will not try to 'take you for a ride.' You will only get quality birds if you are prepared to pay for these. There are rarely bargains in this sort of stock.

As most good breeders are exhibitors, and vice

This budgie is being trained to step onto a stick. Once he learns how to do this, he can be trained to step onto his keeper's finger.

versa, you should seek out those breeders who are already winning consistently with their stock, and at specialty budgerigar shows rather than at shows that cater for many species and stage budgerigar classes with these. The more successful a breeder is, the more you must expect to pay for promising youngsters, or stock that is already winning. You cannot learn to select exhibition stock from reading a book, only from experience. It is thus a case of trying to find a good exhibitor who will take you under his wing (pardon the pun!) and guide you.

Practical Breeding

Budgerigars can be bred either on a colony system or in pairs, depending on your objectives. They can be bred in cages and they will breed throughout the year providing they have about 12 or more hours of daylight. This can include artificial light during the winter months. At such times, they may need some heating as well in order to lessen the risk of hens becoming egg bound.

The colony system is, of course, the natural way in which these birds would breed. Its drawback is that you have no control over which birds pair up, and this is important if you wish to practice controlled breeding for type or given colors. The number of eggs that survive to maturity may also be somewhat lower than with controlled breeding. Conversely, the time you need to devote to the birds, and the cost of breeding, is much lower: this may compensate for the slightly reduced production.

You can also breed budgerigars in a mixed aviary situation though this is not usually recommended because hen budgerigars are rather unpredictable in their attitude to other species in the aviary. They will often attack the eggs or chicks of breeding finches, and few are able to fend off the budgerigar: cockatiels, however, will rarely let budgies (or even larger parakeets) interfere with their nests.

Whichever system of breeding you may decide upon, you should consider two important aspects.

There is little point in breeding with anything other than sound typical birds. Your objective must be to try and breed better birds, rather than simply to breed birds for breeding's sake. You should also consider if you have the outlets to dispose of surplus youngsters and if you have the facility to accommodate them in the event you cannot sell them.

If you plan to breed exhibition-quality stock, then you must obtain birds of high quality from the outset, and they must carry the national club's official legbands. For pet-quality stock this is not important — but you should still breed from good birds.

BREEDING FACTS

Before discussing the procedure of practical breeding, it is worthwhile detailing the breeding facts of budgerigars so they are all in one place for easy reference. Budgerigars are sexually mature when only a few months old, but it is unwise to breed from these birds. Wait until they are at least 12-18 months of age, by which time they will be physically more able to cope with the rigors of rearing clutches of eggs. Although you will hear of breeders who extol the virtues of breeding from under-one-year-old hens, there is little merit in this. Such birds will invariably suffer in later seasons — which is no doubt why a number of breeders claim young hens have given of their best at two years of age. This just is not so if the hen is only bred from when she is fully mature in the first place.

Facing page: A gray pied and a violet. Budgies under one year of age should not be bred, as this is too physically demanding for them.

Mutual preening is part of budgerigar courting behavior. Budgies are noted for forming strong pair bonds, and not uncommonly, if a pair is split up, each bird may be reluctant to accept a new partner.

The cock's breeding life is rather longer than that of the hen, in that the older the hen the higher the number of infertile eggs. Exhibition breeders will normally concentrate on birds that are 2 to 4 years old, as this corresponds with the largest fertile egg production period. However, birds of 7 or more years of age are still able to breed. The number of eggs in a typical clutch will be 4 to 6: the extremes are 0 to 2 and 7 to 9. The number of eggs that will hatch to produce chicks that survive to adults will be about 50% of those laid. Infertility is quite common in budgerigars, more so in cage-bred birds than those given access to aviaries. The incubation period is 17 to 18 days, depending on the weather. The extra day or so is more likely if the temperature falls. The hen incubates the eggs, which are laid on alternate days, but the cock often joins her for various periods of time. The cock will feed the sitting hen. The chicks fledge (leave the nest) when they are 4 to 5 weeks of age. They are then fed by the cock for maybe another week or so, by which time they are independent of their parents, able to feed themselves, and ready to be sold. By the time the chicks have fledged (and maybe a

A budgerigar clutch can be as small as two or as large as nine, but the average is between four and six.

short while before this), the hen will commence laying a second round of eggs.

The chicks are leg banded when they are 4 to 5 days of age (6 to 7 days if they are very small). They cannot be sexed until they have molted into adult plumage at about 3 to 4 months of age (but certain chicks can be sexed once feathers are evident, if they are the product of certain sex-linked color matings.)

Budgerigars form quite strong pair bonds. If a breeding pair are producing good chicks, it is best to keep them together. Once a pair are split they may take some time before they will accept another partner, which is one reason why infertility is rather high in these birds.

BREEDING CONDITION

This is the term used to describe birds that are mentally and physically ready to breed. If both of a pair are not in this condition, the chances are they will fail to produce fertile eggs, the hen will have problems, or the chicks will be sickly and lack vigor. To bring budgerigars into full condition, they should receive plenty of time in an aviary and a steady increase in the protein content of their diet. Some breeders will separate the sexes for many weeks before the breeding season. Others prefer to leave them together in the stock flights until 2 to 3 weeks before the season. They are then separated and selection of pairs is made. If a bird has only recently recovered from a bad illness, it is unwise to breed from it. Try later in the season, or the following season if the latter is already well underway. If you plan to breed in

This is just one of the styles of nestboxes that can be used for budgies.

outdoor aviaries, do not place nestboxes into the flight until you are real sure the risk of freezing weather has passed — this usually means the spring.

NESTBOXES

There are numerous styles of nestboxes used for budgerigars that can be purchased from pet shops. A typical size would be 23cm long by 15cm wide and 15cm deep (9x6x6in). The 23cm could also be the height, so the other two dimensions would then be the width and breadth. Some boxes will have a removable wooden slide at one end, with a glass slide inside this. Such an arrangement allows you to inspect the nest without the risk of the chicks falling out. If the nest box is of the tall type, this could either have a hinged lid, or it could be a lidless box within a box that can be easily pulled out for viewing.

Within the nestbox a loose concave is usually inserted. This is a block of hollowed wood about an inch thick. It helps to keep the eggs together in the center of the box, thus safe from being accidentally pushed to the outer edges where they may not be incubated. The hollow may be central or somewhat towards one end so that when the birds enter the nest they are less likely to scatter the eggs. A landing perch is placed just below the entrance hole, which is placed to one end of the long nestbox or to one side of center in the taller models.

You do not have to use a concave: you may prefer to imitate nature and place about 5cm (2in) of chemically untreated wood shavings into the base of the nestbox. This absorbs the liquid fecal matter of the chicks and, arguably, keeps them cleaner — especially around the legs and between the leg and the legband, if this is fitted. If this method is adopted, it is wise to ensure the base of the nestbox is thick so it will not rot away as quickly as might be the case if it is only of thin wood.

Nestboxes used in

Budgerigar parents and their brood. In general, most budgies are good parents, but there are some whose parenting skills are less than adequate.

birdrooms can be made of plywood, but those to be sited in the aviary should be of thicker wood so they provide insulation on those colder nights. If cage breeding, the nestbox is placed over a hole outside of the cage front. Some fronts are made with the hole already cut out of the wire, but in others you will have to do this yourself — making sure that there are no jagged edges protruding from the cut wires.

When colony breeding, you should hang up more

nestboxes than there are pairs; otherwise, squabbling will almost certainly ensue. Once the birds have paired up, it is wise to remove any unpaired birds, especially hens, as these can create havoc entering nests and generally disturbing the paired birds. After the birds have selected a nestbox you can remove the extra boxes. Try to ensure that the boxes are all placed at about the same height, so none have greater appeal than others, and space them a few feet apart so each pair have their own territory around the box. They should be positioned under a covered part of the flight so they are well protected from inclement weather. On no account should pairs be added to a colony once breeding is underway, as this is a recipe for disaster.

I might mention that plastic nestboxes are now made commercially. Whilst appreciating that plastics do help the mass production market, thus keep costs down, I think there are very definite limits to their application. Plastic sweats in hot weather and provides no insulation in cold weather, so has no value to the bird breeder. Further, parrots enjoy nibbling on the entrance holes, as well as on the inner edges of the boxes. It is emotionally beneficial that they can do this — stick with wood and you cannot go far wrong.

THE PAIRINGS

When selecting a pair, avoid doubling up on any obvious faults. Likewise, do not pair birds that are extremes for given features. A very large bird should not be paired to one that is rather undersized. In this case, either of the birds should be mated to one that

When selecting budgies for a breeding program, their overall soundness and condition should be the most important elements in your choice.

is of the desired size. Health and proven vigor should outweigh any other attribute a bird might have. Known feather pluckers and egg eaters should not be used for breeding until it has been firmly established that their problem was either environmental or nutritional in origin.

The objective is to pair birds that most complement

each other. This does not mean the best cock to the best hen: such matings rarely result in the best chicks, which invariably come from lesser pairings, but in which the birds are probably more complementary to each other. If you plan to breed for given color combinations, you must study the genetics of color. Do not pair two unproven youngsters together. It is always wiser to place an unproven bird with one that has reared chicks before.

INTRODUCING THE PAIRS

As with any aspect of budgerigar breeding, there is no one way that is a sure fire better bet than all others — though breeders of one method will categorically tell you their way is the best! Let us look at the possibilities.

1. You can introduce the cock bird to the aviary or cage first. After a day or two the hen can be introduced and two or more nestboxes can be placed in position. You could place the nestboxes in first if you wish.

2. You can introduce the pair to the breeding quarters at the same time.

3. You can place the hen in the breeding quarters first and allow her to settle down and inspect the nest before you introduce the cock.

4. You can introduce the hen into a double breeder cage with a wire partition separating her from the cock. When they clearly seem interested in each other, you can remove the partition. The advocates of each method will say the other methods fail because the cock might attack the hen, or because the hen will refuse to mate the cock if

she has settled into a nestbox before the cock's introduction. Each of these reasons is based on factual experience, but there can be many reasons why that situation came about. A hen may refuse to be mated if she has taken up residence in a nestbox situated in a small cage — she is less likely to do so in a large cage or an aviary.

Budgerigars are individuals, a fact many breeders often forget. They do not always do what is expected of them, or what the book says they should do. You will hear breeders say they put all of their birds down to nest during this or that week in a given season. This is ridiculous because it assumes all of the pairs are in breeding condition at the same time, which is rarely the case.

Likewise, you will be told that if pairs do not go about the business of mating and egg laying within seven, ten or whatever number of days, they are best split up and tried with new partners. Such comments are human parameters based on the needs of the breeder, rather than the personalities and environment of the pairs involved. Clearly, if a pair do not appear compatible, or if three or more weeks have elapsed and nothing has happened, you must consider the possibility that this pair was not meant for each other, or one or both are not in breeding condition. Never become too dogmatic in your attitude to breeding or any other aspect of budgerigar owning — it stifles progress and the willingness to accept that which may not seem the norm to you, yet is to your birds.

EGGLAYING AND INCUBATION

If all goes well, you can expect a pair to produce eggs within about 14 days. The first two eggs may be laid on consecutive days, though normally the hen lays on alternate days and the chicks will hatch out likewise. However, the hen may not sit in earnest until the second egg is laid, so hatching will not commence until about 19-21 days after the first egg was laid. The hen normally does all of the incubating, and the cock will feed her and will join her in the nest for variable lengths of time, or will sit on a perch close to the nest — or on top of the nestbox.

Although many breeders like to 'candle' the eggs after a few days, usually 6-10, to see if they are developing, this is not necessary. Candling is a term coined by poultry breeders of yesteryear whereby they held an egg in front of a hole behind which was a candle. It allowed the egg contents to be seen. These days a pencil flashlight will do the job and without the need to

An average-size budgie clutch. Especially for the novice breeder, it is very tempting to inspect the eggs. However, the eggs are best left undisturbed until they hatch.

remove the eggs from the nest. Simply shine the light on the eggs. An opaque mass will indicate a fertile egg. If the egg is 'clear,' this means it is infertile. You can often tell which are fertile simply by their color — the clear eggs having an almost transparent look to them.

The first-time breeder is advised to leave well enough alone and not interfere with the nest once it has been established eggs have been laid, until they are due to hatch. If none hatch well after the time they were due, then the clutch can be discarded and the hen will lay her second round. These will usually be fertile. It is not uncommon for the first round of the season to be clear, or the first round of eggs of a maiden hen to be infertile.

CHICK REARING

In the build-up to the

Newborn budgie and eggs that are about to hatch. Note the hole in the egg at the top, where the chick has started to peck its way out of its shell.

breeding season, the pairs of birds will have been given an increase in the protein part of their diet. This should continue throughout the chick-rearing period. Extra calcium is also essential in order to ensure the youngsters develop good strong bone. When the chicks are about five days old, you can fit closed legbands to them. These are

A pair of budgerigars inspecting their nestbox. The perch below the entrance hole makes it easy for the parents to check and see that all is well inside the nestbox.

Newborn budgies are born almost naked and blind. Their eyes do not open until several days after they are born.

obtained from any avicultural supplier. They carry your identification number and a year date. Apart from closed bands or rings, you can purchase split rings. These can be fitted to the chicks (or adults) at any time and serve for temporary identification, such as on youngsters being retained or those that have been sold and so on. They are available in a range of single or double colors.

To fit a closed ring, you must gently turn the chick on its back in your hand. Hold the leg to be ringed with your thumb and index finger and slide the ring over the three longest toes. The fourth toe is then gently pressed backwards and the ring is slipped over this. You may need a toothpick or sharpened matchstick to ease this short toe through the ring. The ring should then dangle freely on the leg. If the ring is too large to stay on, try a day or two later. Much will depend on the size of the chick.

If you have no intentions of exhibiting your budgerigars, it is not that important that they be closed banded. Once fitted, you should check the band on a regular basis. It can easily become clogged with excrement and cause a restriction in the flow of blood to the toes. If clogging occurs, you should dampen the offending dirt so it is soft before gently removing it. In the event that a band should for any reason become tight on a bird's leg, you should take the bird to your vet, who will remove it using a special tool. If this is not done, there is the obvious risk that the bird could loose its foot due to restricted blood flow, gangrene and the like.

When you are attending to the banding is an opportune time to clean the nestbox, if it is dirty. Take the concave out and supply a fresh clean one. Soak the dirty one in a mild solution of disinfectant, and then rinse it before letting it dry thoroughly. If you have used wood shavings, these can be removed (if they are dirty enough to warrant

These babies have already started to grow their downy outer covering. At approximately five weeks of age, they will be completely feathered.

this) and replaced with clean shavings.

You could also take this opportunity to weigh the chicks and so build up a record of weights at differing stages of the chicks' growth. Any loss over the first few weeks would suggest a possible problem because they should gain weight daily until about fledging time, when they may loose just a little. This will quickly be replaced over the following days and until they are mature, at which time their weight will level out. You should also check that there is no build-up of hardened food under the beak of a chick. This sometimes occurs and if left unattended may result in the beak becoming malformed in its growth. Any clogged food can be very gently removed using a toothpick.

Some hens are rather sloppy in attending to cleaning chores, others are excellent. It is useful to add notes on this aspect to the stud card of the hen. It may be the diet that creates a rather wet nest, but it may also be within the hen's genetic make-up. When considering motherhood as a trait, do remember that any weakness in this may have been inherited from the cock's line and not necessarily from the hen's mother. Other than attending to the cleaning of the nest as is required, you should have no further duties with regard to the chicks until they leave the nest. For about a week or so after this time the cock will usually continue to feed them. By the age of about 5 to 6 weeks they should be independent of their parents and can be removed to a separate flight cage or aviary. If there are one or two more "advanced" chicks, or even an adult, being housed along with the newcomers, this will be beneficial. Chicks learn much by imitating their elders, so they will learn to peck and generally do what the older birds do, and eat what they see them eating. Continue to supply some softfood, soaked seed, and similar items until the chicks are clearly taking a wide range of dry seeds.

Sometimes, cocks or hens may attack first-round chicks if the hen is underway with a second round. Watch out for this and remove the chicks if this should occur. Likewise, if a hen starts to unduly pluck the feathers of her chicks, you should try and foster them to a known reliable pair. Such feather plucking may be of genetic origin, in which case the offenders should not be bred from in the future. The problem may, however, indicate a stressed hen, or one that is lacking something in the diet. You must try to find the reason and remedy this.

prolific breeders and this they no doubt are — unless you happen to be the one who runs into trouble. Then you may hear yourself saying 'millions of budgies in the country and I get this pair!' Take heart, you are not alone; all breeders have trouble at some time or other. This is because budgerigars are living entities, not machines that produce fertile eggs to order. In most instances the problems likely to be met with can be solved; others may defy explanation and may disappear at the next breeding attempt. Here we can review the more common problems and hopefully suggest their probable cause and the ways they may be rectified.

BREEDING CONSIDERATIONS

Budgerigars are always regarded as being very

FAILURE TO MATE AND INFERTILITY

These are not uncommon problems in budgerigars,

especially in exhibition stock. It must first be stated that even in wild birds only a percentage of all eggs laid will be fertile, though the percentage will be greater than in captive domesticated stocks, such as budgerigars. There are many reasons for failed matings and infertility. Often it is the degree of infertility that concerns most breeders, rather than total infertility. In such cases the problem often lies in the actual stock used, which has possibly been bred from birds that were not reliable producers. The more likely causes of failed matings and total infertility are:

1. Incompatible pairs. If a pair of breeding budgies are split up in order to effect more desirable matings, this may prompt both of the pair to refuse their next mates (your choice not theirs!). Given time, new pairs may settle down and accept each other. When pair bonds have been established in flight aviaries, it is not unreasonable that when the birds are then placed in breeding cages with new partners they may refuse these. Some breeders keep the sexes apart when the birds are in aviaries for this very reason — to reduce the chance of pairs becoming established until the breeding season. It does not always work.

2. One or both of a pair are not in breeding condition. This is probably more common than is generally thought. Do not place birds into breeding aviaries or cages just because everyone else is doing so at that time of the year — nor because that is when you want your birds to breed. If they are fit and ready, then, and only then, is the time to let them enter nestboxes. Obese or

Budgie parents keeping a watchful eye over their babies. Successful breeding requires much forethought on the part of the hobbyist.

underfed birds are obviously not likely to be in breeding condition.

3. Poor environmental conditions. If the birds are subjected to regular or irregular disturbances that are of a stressful nature, or frightening, you cannot expect them to breed. This may happen in mixed collection or colony aviaries where other birds intimidate the pair, or one of the pair. It can happen if larger parrots occupy an adjacent or nearby aviary — or if dogs, cats or, more often, birds of prey are in the immediate vicinity. The pair may eventually get used to these potential dangers, but they may never do so, it being very much an individual matter. If the problem is with aviary birds, give them a try in an indoor flight or cage.

4. One of the pair may have a genetic or reproductive problem that renders them infertile. This is a possibility with any bird that has never been bred before. This does not mean that the hen cannot lay eggs, just that such eggs were never capable of being fertilized.

5. Anatomical defect. If a cock or hen cannot grasp the perch properly, this is likely to result in a failed mating. This may be the result of a missing toe, a claw, or a broken limb that has not set in the correct position. I will include excessive feathering under this heading. Buff feathered birds have coarse feathers that may obstruct the vent area of one of the pair. Remove any feathers that seem excessive around the vent area. Also, check the feathers of the thighs, which may also be implicated even in non-buff birds.

6. In the case of birdroom breeders, the temperature may be too high or two low. It may fluctuate wildly. Check it and also consider how much artificial light is available; maybe you do not leave the lights on long enough. The birds will need 12-14 hours of daylight or its equivalent before they are induced to breed.

7. Lack of vigor. This can be viewed in two ways. If you breed excessively from a pair, they will eventually be physically drained and incapable of producing viable sperm or ova as the case may be. Genetically, the birds may be the result of a long line of pairings in which beauty, rather than breeding vigor, was the all-important reason the birds were kept. Such policies are as barren as the birds they eventually yield. Be sure the pair are from a good vigorous line before you

An assortment of young budgerigars in various stages of development.

purchase them. The fact that they are from an inbred line does not of itself imply lack of vigor.

8. Effect of medications. If a bird has recently recovered from an illness that was treated with modern drugs, it is possible these may have affected the bird's reproductive glands, rendering it infertile. This condition could be temporary or permanent and only your vet can advise on the likelihood of this.

EGGS THAT FAIL TO HATCH

The most common cause of budgerigar eggs failing to hatch is because they are infertile, a fact established by careful studies into the problem. This leaves failures due to other causes, of which there are many.

1. The hen may be in a fearful or stressed state. As a result, she may leave the nest frequently, or not sit tight on the eggs. The cock may disturb her a great deal, as might chicks from a previous round that are still in the nest. If the nest contains parasites, such as red mite, these might really unsettle her, so she again leaves the nest frequently, or may even abandon the eggs.

2. The clutch may be too large for the hen to cope with, and certain eggs may get pushed to the outer edge of the nestbox where they become chilled. This is obviously more likely in aviaries where breeding has commenced too early or too late in the season, when the temperature falls below the desired optimums. Also, the hen may simply be a poor mother.

3. The egg may be damaged by accident. For example, if you handle the eggs, you may cause a hairline crack through which bacteria can enter the embryo and kill it. The hen or the cock could do likewise with their claws, or even their legbands. The first chicks to hatch could also damage the last eggs to be laid. Sometimes you can repair a crack by using nail varnish — it's always worth a try.

4. The embryo may have received pathogenic bacteria directly from the hen at the time of its conception or could have inherited a lethal gene that prevents it from developing beyond the egg stage.

5. The environmental humidity may be too low or too high. In the former case,

Budgerigar nestlings. The spine-like feathers that are visible will soon be replaced by smooth plumage.

the egg dries up; in the latter the egg is unable to shed excess moisture, so the forming chick is drowned.

6. The eggshell is too thick, the chick is too weak to break through the shell, or maybe a combination of both. In the latter case, this would suggest that the hen was herself undernourished and incapable of passing sufficient food to the developing egg before it became an independent unit. I have been asked from time to time what the effect of hard water intake is on the structure of the eggshell — does it become too hard

for chicks to break clear of? Regrettably, I cannot answer this with any factual data.

However, the birds of breeders living in hard water areas do not seem to suffer as a result of the state of the water. Further, given the wide distribution of the wild budgerigar, it must be assumed they drink in areas of hard water and that this does not affect the strength of the shell such that it would prevent the chicks from breaking through.

PIPPED EGGS

This term is used to describe an egg in which the chick has managed to make a small hole in the shell with its egg tooth (a hard growth on the upper beak that disappears some time after the chick has freed itself from the egg) but is unable to make further progress. Leave the egg for 24 hours. If the chick has still not cleared itself of the egg, you can very carefully pull small pieces of the shell away from the area of the hole. If the membrane covering is tough, you can equally carefully snip it a little. Leave matters for a few hours and see if the chick emerges. If not, remove a little more of the shell to free the chick, dabbing its navel with a suitable antiseptic lotion. Hopefully, it will survive — though this is not always the case.

EGGBINDING

When a hen is unable to pass an egg, she is said to be eggbound. The condition is very distressing to her and can be fatal if you do not react quickly. You will notice an eggbound hen because her lower abdomen will be inflated and she will often flutter to the ground and seek a quiet corner where she will strain to shed the problem egg. The condition has numerous causes.

1. An egg may be oversized and simply too big for the hen to shed it.

2. If the hen is obese, or out of condition, her muscles do not contract and relax in the correct rhythm. They may contract behind and in front of the egg at the same time — so the egg remains in place. They may also be contracting too weakly, thus not pushing the egg enough to clear the vent, where it meets more resistance than farther back in the oviduct.

3. The egg may have a very soft shell (as the result of a calcium or other nutritional deficiency). As the muscles contract, the egg simply gives way, so it fails to move forward.

4. The hen may be chilled, so is unable to contract her muscles correctly.

5. The oviduct walls may themselves be in bad health. As a result their linings become swollen and thus the egg cannot make progress.

6. The hen has simply become exhausted from being bred from too often. There can be other physiological reasons for eggbinding, but they all result in the egg's being unable to proceed down the oviduct. Old ideas on how to deal with the problem include gently applying olive or other oil to the vent area and then holding the hen over steam in order to relax the muscles. The problem is that oils will clog the feathers and reduce the insulating effect of these. Thus the hen may become chilled more than she may already be. The steam, of course, could scald her and will certainly frighten her.

The most reliable method is to place the hen in a heated cage. More often than not this will induce her to pass the egg, as it will supply general heat without the risk of scalding or frightening her. If this has failed after an hour or so, you can either contact your vet or try very gently(!) to manipulate the egg out. Should the egg break inside of her oviduct, it could cause peritonitis, a very dangerous infection of the whole body cavity. If in doubt, rush her to the vet after first phoning for his or her advice. Once the egg is cleared the hen may lay the rest of the clutch without problem. However, it would be as well to foster the eggs to another hen and let the eggbound hen fully recover her strength in an indoor cage or her regular aviary if the weather is warm. Do not breed her until the next season — and never again if there is any chance that the problem is of a genetic base. You can establish the latter fact only if you know that

Budgies experience a rapid rate of growth and development. They are fully independent by the age of six weeks.

the conditions she lives under are good and if you have the records that would suggest it is more than chance that her 'line' seems to produce a higher than normal incidence of eggbound hens.

FOSTERING EGGS AND CHICKS

One of the advantages of having a number of pairs breeding at about the same time is that eggs or chicks can be fostered if the need arises. Do not place eggs under a foster hen that already has enough eggs to cope with. Some breeders will put up one or two pairs to breed even though they do not want the eggs from them. In this way, they know they can dispose of such a pair's eggs should the need arise for them to foster eggs of a good pair.

Budgie hen and her chicks. The hen lays her eggs at various intervals; thus, all the chicks do not hatch at the same time.

A basic knowledge of genetic principles is very helpful in structuring a breeding program.

Understanding Genetics

The subject of genetics is an area of many animal hobbies that breeders do not always wish to study, yet find time and again they have a need to understand it. This is especially so in budgerigars, where there are more color permutations to work with than in other pets, koi being the possible exception. Once you have mastered the basic principles of heredity, you may find you are hooked on the subject. Even if you do not, it will widen your horizons in terms of breeding philosophy.

THE LIMITATIONS OF GENETICS

Before looking at some basic genetic principles, it is worthwhile pondering the limitations of this science. Clearly, many breeders over the centuries have managed to produce superb stock without any knowledge of the science, which is relatively new. However, such people were using genetic principles even if they did not realize it. They were simply good breeders. This implies a number of attributes that are not directly involved in heredity. The genes of an animal give it a very fixed potential, but whether or not it realizes this potential is governed by numerous other facets of its life.

1. Nutrition. The development of a budgerigar is the end product of a long chain of chemical reactions. The fuel for these is, of course, the food eaten. Any deficiency in this must be reflected in a lack of growth. This will

totally mask the genetic virtues of the bird in question. This is especially so where color is concerned; poor food can only result in faded looking colors. The genetic potential of the bird might be tremendous, but how are you to know this if it looks a mediocre bird of washed out color? The use of coloring agents in foods is a poor substitute for sound nutrition because it is a temporary means of making the mediocre look rather better than its genetic state.

2. Environment. The living conditions of a bird will greatly affect its health, and thus its potential. Overcrowding will result in a high risk of poor health. The birds will not gain the full value of the food they are given, even if this is of an excellent standard. Poor accommodation will result in birds that are stressed, and a stressed bird simply will not develop or eat as it should.

Aviary birds that have no protection from strong sunlight will never display full color because the sun will bleach the pigments and make them paler. This does not mean they should be kept for long periods in birdrooms where they will neither gain the benefit of the sun, nor the many advantages of being in an outdoor environment. The latter is absolutely crucial to birds in order that they retain vigorous health.

The environmental factor extends into the breeding room in relation to breeding cages. Budgerigars are flock, thus social, birds by nature. When they cannot see or hear others of their kind, this will lower the reproductive urge and may stress them.

It is therefore wise to arrange cages in a facing

manner, rather than in a line. Alternatively, the use of wire partitions between cages, rather than solid wood, is one method of overcoming the problems related to the need for the birds to see, as well as to hear, each other.

SELECTION

Genetics without selection is of no value whatsoever. Survival of wild budgerigars is dependent on natural selection. In a breeding stud, the whole success of the line being developed is

An opaline cock, cinnamon yellow-green hen, and their offspring, who are replicas of their mother.

Very often a breeder may attribute breeding failure to the genetic state of the bird, or a lack of something in the diet, when the reality is that the full influence of the total environment is not given the value that it should be given.

dependent on the breeder consistently making the correct selections from the birds available to him or her. This obviously entails having an intimate knowledge of budgerigars, an eye for that special bird — and a modicum of good luck, the latter of which should never be underrated. It should be added that the value of 'an eye' is questionable and sometimes overrated. Those people who are regarded as having this natural attribute are usually those who have also devoted a tremendous amount of time to studying their chosen subjects.

The keeping of detailed breeding records is essential to any person attempting to make selections from birds. If we humans have a weakness, it is that we do not always appreciate that our memory is rather suspect. Records greatly overcome this problem!

THE VALUE OF GENETIC STUDY

Understanding how heredity works increases a breeder's chances of achiev-ing many objectives. It can save a great deal of wasted pairings, especially where easily observed features like color are concerned. You can work out what your chances are of obtaining given colors and may thus proceed — or decide the odds are too long. No specific genes are identified in relation to conformation, but knowing how they work enables a breeder to steadily improve his stock without the risk of suddenly putting that progress in jeopardy by introducing outcrosses. If you appreciate what this could mean, it will prompt you to take a cautious path that protects any progress you have made.

Likewise, if you understand the benefits and negatives of inbreeding, the latter term will no longer be as frightening as it often is to the uninformed. Genetics is not the be-all and end-all of good breeding but is just another tool in the work kit. Used wisely it will help you; used badly you will gain nothing from its application.

GENES AND CHROMOSOMES

All the features of a budgerigar are passed from one generation to the next by genes. These are tiny units of coded information that tell each cell how it will develop. They are held together on chains called chromosomes. Each species has a characteristic number of chromosomes, the budgerigar having 26. These are made up of 13 pairs, of which one pair are termed sex chromosomes. When budgerigars mate, each bird passes one of its paired chromosomes to its offspring; these are within the zygote that will develop into the embryo and thus the chick.

Each chromosome from the parent bird will carry half of the genes the parent had itself received. The youngster thus inherits two chromosomes, thus the paired situation is restored. The position at which any one gene is located is called its locus (pl.loci), so for any one feature there will be two genes (the exception being in the sex cells).

Few features are controlled by a single gene, and color is no exception. Many loci are involved — how many is not known because a gene can only be identified as a unit when it mutates. When this happens, it can be named and studied in the way it is passed on. This information can then be used to forecast how it will affect the color of the bird that carries it.

MUTATION

Genes express themselves

in a very predictable manner for most of the time. However, every so often a gene will suddenly change the information it gives to the cells it is in. It is said to have mutated. If the mutant gene proves beneficial to the animal carrying it, then the gene will spread through the species; if not it will die out. Generally, mutations are not beneficial so they die out — to happen again many years later when conditions may favor their retention. New species are created by the effect of mutation over millions of years. Not all mutations are dramatic and many are not even noticed over short spans of time — like a few hundred years. Breeders only notice major mutations — especially when they affect some very visible feature, such as feather structure or color, or when they are associated with an abnormal problem that is undesirable.

Under captive conditions, we can, of course, retain mutations if they are pleasing. They can be improved because most genes are associated with what are called modifying genes. The latter are numerous and result in the expression of the major gene being modified within a given range. For example, a green budgerigar can be many shades of green, all that little bit different. By continually breeding from darker greens, a stud will eventually establish that shade. Another breeder may select from only the lighter shades. Size, it is thought, is determined by selection for genes that show themselves on a build-up basis.

I should add that in discussing green, you cannot obtain an olive green by selection for modifiers

It is easy to see how this type of budgerigar, a feather duster, earned its name. The long feathers greatly inhibit the bird's ability to function and some of these birds are barely able to see.

because that color is beyond the normal range of these. Olive green is created by another gene mutation, but if this is carried by a budgerigar it can then appear a lighter or darker shade depending on selection for modifiers. It can get very difficult to tell if a bird is carrying certain major genes or whether it is the result of selection for these modifying genes. The subject can get extremely complicated as you delve further into it.

Once a mutation has occurred, the gene in question is named, as already mentioned. For example, an early mutation in budgerigars was one that prevented the development of yellow pigment. The result was the arrival of the skyblue color. The gene was designated the letter b to stand for blue. Why genes mutate is not fully understood, and many experiments to induce mutation have failed to establish a cause. They are not common, appearing only when animals are bred in extremely large numbers.

GENETIC TERMINOLOGY

In any study field there is a need to use special words to convey a given meaning. In genetics, many such words are used so you will need to learn a number of these. Furthermore, in order to make breeding calculations easy to do, geneticists use a sort of shorthand. We can introduce words and shorthand by looking at the results of a mating between a green and a blue budgerigar. All of the chicks will be green, assuming the green parent is pure for its color (you will understand the meaning of this shortly).

The reason the chicks are green is because certain genes have more power to express themselves than others. Such genes are said to be dominant to the other type, which are said to be recessive. Dominant genes are indicated in calculations by assigning them a capital letter; recessive genes use a lowercase letter. In order to indicate that contrasting genes at the same locus are alternatives to each other,

Two well-known color varieties of budgerigar: the green and cobalt blue.

bb. Each parent can pass only one of its genes to its offspring, so it follows that all of the offspring will have the genotype of Bb. As green is dominant, the chicks in this instance are described as green split for blue. This is written as green/blue; that in front of the line is visual, that behind is carried and not seen. Birds having contrasting genes at a given locus are said to be heterozygous — non-purebreeding for that feature. If both genes are the same, as in the BB and bb parents, they are homozygous, or pure for that feature.

the alternative gene to the mutant one will carry the same letter. Were this not done, you might easily forget that one was the alternative to the other.

Given this information, the green parent can be designated BB, and the blue

PAIRING HETEROZYGOTES

If the first-generation birds were to be paired with others of the same genotype, the results, which are interesting, can be shown as follows: Bb x Bb = BB, Bb, bB, and bb. Can you see how the calculations are made? The B of the one parent can combine with either the B or the b of the other bird. Likewise, the b of the first parent can unite with either the B or the b of the other bird. You must work out every possible combination to arrive at the theoretical expectations because it is random chance which genes will combine with which. If the expectations are converted into colors they will be as follows: 1 Green BB (Homozygous), 2 Green Bb and bB (Heterozygous), and 1 Blue bb (Homozygous).

There is no visual difference between the two sorts of green birds. The only way you would be able to find out which was which would be to pair one of them to a blue. If any blue chicks appeared in the clutch, this would prove the green bird was split for this color, because the only way that chick could have received its blue color was through a blue gene from each parent. Thus: Bb x bb = Bb, Bb, bb, and bb. Your chance of a blue chick is therefore 50/50. Had the green bird been the homozygous genotype, you would, of course, have obtained only green/blue chicks by pairing the green to a blue bird. It is important that you do not assume that because no blue chicks appear this would confirm that the green parent must have been homozygous — this has not been established at this point for the reason to be discussed next.

RANDOM COMBINATION OF GENES

The hen will produce many eggs (ova) and the cock will produce millions

A gene that masks the characteristic of another gene is said to be dominant; the gene that is masked is termed recessive.

of sperm. The ova and sperm will each contain one of the genes for a given feature, but it is a matter of chance which sperm will fertilize which ovum. The budgerigar only produces an average of 4 to 6 chicks per clutch, so it is possible for these to be all green, all blue, or any combination of these — the chance being that which has been theoretically calculated.

The pairing of heterozygotes illustrates that recessive genes only show themselves if they are in double dose, whereas a dominant gene need only be present in a single form to express itself visually. This pairing also shows that a green bird can be regarded in two distinct ways. There is its external appearance, called its phenotype, and the genetic state that made that appearance, its genotype.

You will appreciate the importance of this fact in that if you do not know the genotype of a given bird, you could find yourself with a lot of chicks of unwanted colors if they were carrying recessive genes in their make-up. Equally so, if you know a bird is split for a desired color, you also know you can produce that color with a selected breeding program.

The gene actions discussed are termed autosomal dominant and autosomal recessive, meaning they are genes found in the body (somatic) cells of the bird. As such, the sex of the budgerigar has no bearing on the outcome of any pairing involving these genes, so it does not matter which parent has the dominant or recessive genes. Their combination can therefore appear in either cocks or hens. The following genes are autosomal recessives in the budgerigar (you can work out pairings by simply substituting them for blue in the examples given): Brownwing n, Clearwing c^w, Dilute c^d, Graywing c^g, English gray e, English Fallow f, German Fallow g, Non-sex-linked Ino i, Recessive (Danish) Pied r, Scottish Fallow s, Yellow-Faced Mutant 1 b^y.

PAIRING TWO RECESSIVE MUTATIONS

If two budgerigars are paired and each is the result

of a recessive mutation, you can work out the potential offspring without any problems as long as you bear in mind a simple fact. Let us say you paired a blue cock with an English fallow hen (it doesn't actually matter which color is which sex). Then you might be tempted to work things out as follows: bb x ee = be be be be. This would leave you wondering what the color of the chicks is. What has been overlooked in this calculation is that at the fallow locus the blue bird is non-fallow, whilst at the blue locus the fallow bird is non-blue. In either case, this means the alternative gene to the recessive is that for normal color. The formula is thus: EEbb x eeBB = EeBb. In this instance there is only one potential combination of these genes which is why only one has been shown. All of the chicks are normal

The development of new color varieties is one of the most exciting aspects of the budgerigar hobby.

(green) split for both blue and fallow: normal/blue-fallow. If you look at the genotype of the chicks you will see why. The e and b are in single dose so cannot be seen visually. In each case their dominant alternative gene is for normality, that is, green and non-fallow.

COCK GAMETES

		FB	Fb	fB	fb
	FB	FFBB	FFBb	FfBB	FfBb
HEN	**Fb**	FFBb	FFbb	FfBb	Ffbb
GAMETES	**fB**	FfBB	FfBb	ffBB	ffBb
	fb	FfBb	Ffbb	ffBb	ffbb

PAIRING DOUBLE SPLIT BIRDS

The next calculation we should make is to pair the double split chicks and see what happens. In order to work out the potential offspring, it is convenient to use a Punnett square. Each possible combination of genes is placed along the top and side lines and then you simply fill in the squares. The genes (actually the gametes, which contain the genes) from these split birds are: FfBb = FB Fb fB and fb.

Summarizing the colors of these birds, there are: 9 Normal, 3 Blue, 3 Fallow, and 1 Fallow Blue.

This ratio of 9:3:3:1 is standard when two pairs of contrasting genes are involved. There are no less than 9 genotypes, but only four phenotypes. Of the 16 permutations, just 4 are purebreeding for both of their features — one of each color. If you were to write down the genotype of, for example, one of the normals, bearing in mind you would not know if it was homozygous or heterozygous for green, or whether or not it carried either or both of the recessive genes, it would appear thus: B- F -. In this instance the dashes indicate the unknown genes, assuming you know there is a chance that recessives may be present, which you would in this case given the history of the birds. The blues would appear as bbF because you know they are homozygous for the blue and you know they might be carrying a single fallow gene.

Once again you can appreciate the value of knowing the genotype of birds used because it could save you much wasted time in pairings and clutches in order to find out. Remember, a bird can be carrying (split for) a number of recessives.

INCOMPLETE DOMINANCE

Genes never blend in the way that paint does to create another color. However, it might at times seem that this must be so. If you pair a skyblue to a mauve you will obtain cobalt chicks, which are midway in color between the two parents. The reason this happens is due to an incompletely dominant gene called the dark factor — designated D. The skyblue does not carry this gene so at the dark factor locus it is dd. The mauve carries the factor in double dose so is DD, whilst the cobalt carries one gene for it, so is Dd. You can work out the results involving this gene in the same way as was done for green x blue: dd x DD = Dd (all single factor birds); Dd x Dd = DD Dd dD dd (25% Double Factor, 50% Single Factor, and 25% normal—

Above: A fallow light green (left) and a fallow cobalt. **Below:** A dark-eyed clear white (left) and a lutino. Note how all of these birds differ from each other in head size and body size.

Above: A crested normal cobalt (left) and a half circular crested normal cobalt. **Below:** A tufted normal dark green (left) and a tufted normal skyblue. In good budgie specimens, the throat spots are rounded and evenly spaced.

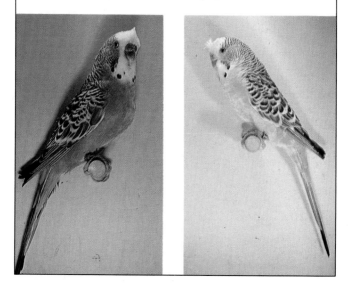

Above: A halfsider recessive pied cobalt (left) and a Dutch pied clearflight light green. **Below:** A quartersider opaline dark green cobalt (left) and an Australian banded pied normal green.

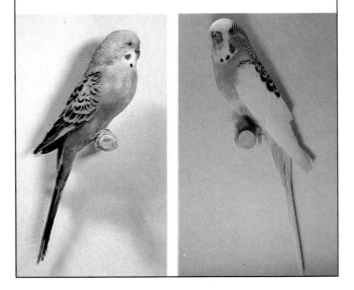

whatever that color may be). (Note: you would normally transpose dD to Dd.)

When applied to other colors the genotypes are: Olive Green DD, Dark Green Dd, Light Green dd, Olive Yellow DD, Dark Yellow Dd, Light Yellow dd, Dark Gray DD, Medium Gray Dd, and Light Gray dd.

It is unfortunate that budgerigar breeders have used the term dark when applied to the mid shades of green and yellow. This is not a situation unique to these birds; similar situations are found in other domestic pets in relation to color terminology.

MIMIC GENES

This term is applied to situations where two or more quite distinct mutations result in the same phenotype. As long as you are aware that this can happen, it will not present problems. In budgerigars, the English, Scottish and German fallows are examples, though the latter can be detected on account of their darker eye color and the presence of a white iris. Superficially, however, the fallows are similar, but if you were to pair an English to a Scottish you might be surprised when none of the chicks were fallow. As long as you appreciate that the mutations are at differing loci there is no problem, as is shown by the expectations from pairing these: SSff x FFss = SsFf = Normal/ English-Scottish Fallow.

DOMINANT MUTATIONS

Whilst most mutations are recessive to the normal wild type, there are a few that are dominant to it. These are indicated by giving them a capital letter.

Thus, the alternative to them, the normal, is given the lowercase. Examples are the Australian gray (A), Violet (V), and Yellow Face Mutant 2 (Y).

SEX DETERMINATION

Whilst all chromosome pairs are identical in the body (somatic) cells, those in the sex cells differ from each other in length. They are designated X and Y. A cock carries two X chromosomes whilst the hen is XY. In any clutch, the chances of an equal number of cocks and hens is theoretically 50/50, as can be seen from the pairing of these: XX x XY = XX XY XX XY. In reality, random chance plays its part, so you could have any ratio of one to the other, or all of one sex.

SEX LINKAGE

In all of the mutations so far considered, the sex of the bird has no influence on the results in terms of the color and the bird carrying it. However, there are four exceptions to this situation. These are the ino (albino and lutino) Xi, the cinnamon Xc, the opaline Xo, and the slate Xs. Note that the color is carried on the X chromosome. The Y chromosome is shorter and has no corresponding color loci to those on its opposite. It is primarily concerned with matters relating to sexual differences. Thus, the hen determines the sex of the chicks, depending on whether or not she passes her chicks an X or a Y chromosome.

The important point with sex-linked colors is that a hen can display the color even though it is recessive and she has only one gene for it. She cannot be split for a sex-linked color as the cock can (but she can still be split for any non-sex-linked colors: remember, they are

1. Normal cock XCXC x Cinnamon hen XcY

	XC	
Xc	XCXc	Normal/Cinnamon cocks (50%)
Y	XCY	Normal hens (50%)

2. Normal/Cinnamon cock XCXc x Normal hen XCY

	XC	Xc	
XC	XCXC	XCXc	Normal cocks (25%) Normal/Cinnamon cocks (25%)
Y	XCY	XcY	Normal hens (25%) Cinnamon hens (25%)

3. Cinnamon Cock XcXc x Normal hen XCY

	Xc	
XC	XCXc	Normal/Cinnamon cocks (50%)
Y	XcY	Cinnamon hens (50%)

4. Normal/Cinnamon cock XCXc x Cinnamon hen XcY

	XC	Xc	
Xc	XcXC	XcXc	Normal/Cinnamon cocks (25%) Cinnamon cocks (25%)
Y	XCY	XcY	Normal hens (25%) Cinnamon hens (25%)

carried on the body cell chromosomes). We can look at how things work out when sex-linked birds are paired to normals.

Cinnamon cocks mated to cinnamon hens will, of course, produce 100% cinnamon chicks. You may note that a cock cinnamon can only be produced if the mother is a cinnamon. Also, if the cock and hen are visually normal but you know (or even if you do not) that the cock carries a sex-linked gene, then any chicks showing the sex-linked color must be hens. Such birds can thus be sexed as soon as their color begins to show.

If you breed a pair of like-colored birds, you are likely to get offspring that resemble their parents.

THE INO GENE

This mutation has the effect of removing all black pigment from the bird carrying it. If it is working on a green bird, it will result in a lutino; if on a blue bird, you will have an albino. An interesting point about the gene is that it is epistatic to all other genes. This means that when you see an albino budgerigar, there is really no way of telling what colors it is masking in its genotype. If you do not quite understand this aspect of masking, then consider the genotype of an albino masking a cobalt cock: bbDdXiXi. The ino gene prevents the black in the blue gene from forming. This means that the dark factor has nothing to work on so therefore has no effect. However, the blue and dark factor genes are still at their loci. If the albino bird carrying them was paired to a normal skyblue hen, then the formula would be as follows: bbDdXiXi x bbddXIY = bbDdXIXi Cobalt/ino cocks (25%), bbddXIXi Skyblue/ino cocks (25%), bbDdXiY Albino/cobalt hens (25%), and bbddXiY Albino/ skyblue hens (25%).

The cocks produced are visually cobalt or skyblue,

showing that both the blue and dark factors are still present, but now they are suppressed in the hens by the ino gene.

LETHAL GENES

A mutant gene may not always be desirable, even if it produces desirable changes. For example the gene that creates a crested budgerigar is lethal in the homozygous state, so all crested budgies are obligate heterozygotes. Such birds are quite normal in all other respects. The lethality is prenatal, so the effect is that the potential clutch size will always be reduced by 25% (theoretically). To appreciate this, we can designate the crest gene as C (it is a dominant mutation): Cc x Cc = CC Cc Cc cc. Transposed this gives us: 25% double factor crested (lethal), 50% Single factor crested, and 25% Non-crested.

Mutations have helped to create a variety of beautifully colored budgerigars.

It should be mentioned that it is now thought that the genotypes of crested budgerigars are rather more complex than indicated here, and two or more genes may be involved in crest production. The usual advice in respect to these birds is clearly to pair crested birds with normals, thus avoiding any lethality in the offspring: Cc x cc = Cc Cc cc cc = 50% crested, 50% normals.

By applying that discussed in this chapter, you can work out a large number of potential matings in order to decide if they are worthwhile, or what they are likely to produce. You should, however, always understand that the genotype might sound more appealing than the reality of this. Likewise, some mutant genes are extremely variable, so that one pied bird could look stunning, another might look pretty pathetic.

GENES AND CONFORMATION

As has been discussed, geneticists can only identify a gene when it mutates. From this it can be seen that where conformation is concerned, nothing is known about the genetic make-up of this. As a result, all formulas for genotypes of given birds are purely in reference to the bird's color, and maybe its crest. It is not known whether a given virtue in a show bird is best in a heterozygous or homozygous state, though most assume the latter.

Lethal genes in livestock clearly illustrate the fact that homozygosity is not always the ideal state, nor are dominant genes. Some features may depend on recessive genes. There is also the fact that certain genes may be linked to others, or to the sex of the

If you are interested in producing a particular color, careful attention must be given to the color and physical characteristics of the prospective breeding pair.

bird. Nonetheless, conclusions can be drawn on breeding programs if you understand genes.

Aspects of Breeding

In this chapter the objective is to look at aspects of breeding systems. If you are aware of the benefits and negatives of pursuing given paths, you will be more able to decide what you feel is the best suited to your particular needs.

INITIAL CONSIDERATIONS

It is important that a novice breeder keeps an open mind on matters relating to breeding philosophy. It can be easy to be influenced by the apparent success of a system that owes as much to the breeder as the system. If breeder A is consistently successful on the show bench, whilst breeder B, using a differing method, is far less so, there is the temptation to assume that breeder A has the better system. This may be so, but it may also be that the breeder has far more ability to make good selections from the stock than breeder B, whose actual system might even be superior. It may also indicate that breeder A started off with better stock in the first place.

In reality, no one system will guarantee you success because all breeding systems are heavily dependent on the crucial aspect of selection, and the basis on which this is made. Nor should you assume that a good breeder is necessarily a good judge of quality exhibition stock. The former requires the application of sound principles that will ensure a steady improvement in the overall standard of the stock. The latter needs an informed eye for the type of bird that will win a show — which by no means suggests it is valuable from a breeding viewpoint, though it is obviously hoped this will be so. The prerequisites of a good breeding bird and a good show bird are not necessarily the same. The one is dependent on genotype, the other on phenotype. The would-be breeder is therefore advised to obtain sound birds of known ancestry, rather than winning birds of uncertain breeding. Clearly, the ideal choice is stock from winning lines of proven ancestry.

SELECTION

Vital to any breeding system is the method by which future breeding stock is evaluated. This implies that the breeder has established the parameters of the objectives, which is not always so. The exhibition breeder is clearly looking for stock that has the potential for winning — which does not mean vigor, disease resistance, longevity, or hatchability are necessarily high on the list of priorities.

If the method of selection is not well thought out, it is unlikely any lasting success will be achieved. If emphasis is placed on trivial matters, and these are rated as equal to major aspects, then many outstanding birds may be overlooked as future breeding stock. It is best to make up a list of the virtues and faults in your stock and then let a good breeder look at the list and advise you of the relevant importance of these. They can then be given a value.

A good way to scale values is to apply a coefficient once the selected features have been established. It would work as follows. Breeding vigor might be given a coefficient of 4, health 3, head shape 3, feather quality 2, color 2, throat spots 2, and other features 1 each. The birds are then judged, based on a point system of 1 to 10 for each of the features, and the score is multiplied by the coefficient. If you rated a given bird's color as 6 points out of 10, this would thus be multiplied by 2 to give 12.

This method ensures that the most important features are given the best chance to score well. Very often, when assessing birds purely on a visual basis without a scoring system, it is possible to get carried away by some outstanding aspect that is actually not so important in the overall needs of the breeder's program. The coefficient safeguards against this. However, this system does mean that the

The requirements for producing a good breeder are not necessarily the same as those for producing a good exhibition bird.

importance of a feature to you must be weighted with much thought and the coefficient values carefully worked out. Once progress is made in a given feature, then its value can be lowered, those of others being raised according to needs. The system is referred to as the total score, or index selection method.

It is superior to that of either tandem selection or independent culling levels because it is more precise in pinpointing the overall worth of any given budgerigar. Tandem selection is when you select for a single feature. This method can bring dramatic results in terms of improvement to a given poor feature. Once the feature is raised in standard, you then select another feature and so on. The problem is that as you improve the second and third features, the first one may regress, so progress is painstakingly slow.

Culling methods work on the basis that you apply a judgment made against given features. You may reject any bird that scores low for certain features, or below an overall score. The drawback to this is that you might reject a bird that fell short on one or two features, even though it scored well on a really needed feature. The system may be compared to that used in judging birds (and many other show animals). It penalizes that which is faulty, but gives no undue credit to that which is outstanding. A bird with the fewest faults is thus kept for breeding, rather than one that has obvious outstanding qualities, but some faults. The total score method is thus more all-embracing in meeting your specific needs.

Progeny testing is another popular means of selecting breeding stock. In this method you are not basing your selection on the appearance of the bird, or on how many wins it has achieved. With progeny testing, you are actually evaluating and deciding breeding worthiness. What happens is that you pair a cock with a number of hens and record the various features important to you. These may be clutch size, health, overall size, size of throat spots, or whatever.

The offspring are graded — maybe by a total score method —and the gross total score of the clutch is divided by the number of chicks to give you an average score. Another cock is then mated to the same hens, and thus another average score is produced. The cock producing the best average is thus the better choice as a breeding bird. The same, of course, would apply to the hens. Indeed, one should always pay as much attention to the hens as much as one does to the cocks; both provide half of a chick's quality (or lack of it).

The cocks must be mated to the same hens, otherwise you will not get a fair comparison. Clearly, some hens will be better than others in their breeding ability. If cocks are compared to each other purely on progeny to any hens, rather than to the same hens, the increased average score of one cock may reflect the superior qualities of the hen rather than those of the cock.

With progeny testing you may often find that the best looking cocks are not the best breeders, a common happening in all animals. Breeding worth and appearance are not always positively correlated. You will appreciate that progeny testing does entail some commitment to given birds before an evaluation can be made. It will entail having foster hens available. These can rear first-round chicks

An albino budgie hen with her two opaline offspring. The other occupants of the nest were two albinos.

so a second round can be undertaken using the second cock, which is paired to the hen previously mated by the other cock. This method of testing is especially valuable for testing features not easily judged by appearance — health, number of eggs produced, breeding vigor, and similar traits.

You will appreciate that in deciding on your methods of selection, you are already undertaking a breeding system of sorts. Many breeders, in truth, have no system as such because they regard the selection process as a system, which it is not in the genetical sense. Selection has only a limited influence on the genetic state of the birds, unless it is associated with a given system. It is valuable in sorting out the best birds from which to commence a more involved program.

FAMILIES AND STRAINS

Talk with budgerigar breeders at any show, or read the avicultural papers, and you will hear or see the terms families and strains tossed about with impunity. Very, very few breeders of budgies can actually claim they have either, though they often do. Both of these terms have specific meanings. They are used to describe groups of birds that have quite distinct features that set them apart from the average of the population. Usually, such features are of an outstanding nature, but this is not necessarily so. A strain may also have some specific physiological features associated with it. Normally, you could only claim a strain or family if it had been inbred for at least six generations.

THE BREEDER'S DILEMMA — MEDIUM AND EXTREME EXPRESSION

One of the major dilemmas confronting you as a breeder is how to overcome the problems created by the need to introduce both medium and extreme expression of genes at one and the same time. The ideal budgerigar is required to have a number of features that are represented by both of these genetic states. Let us consider a hypothetical example — we cannot do otherwise because no one knows the genotype of any aspect of conformation.

You will wish to obtain medium expression in many

features of your birds, such as overall size, wing length, head size, tail length, and so on. By medium is meant not deviating too far towards the potential extremes that may be theoretically possible genetically for a given feature. You want a good-sized bird, not a giant or a dwarf! It should be well proportioned in its make-up. To do this, you need to follow a program of gene fixation. The only way this can be achieved is by inbreeding, to a greater or lesser degree. This implies increasing the homozygotic state of your birds or, put

Breeders try to produce budgies that are well proportioned.

another way, reducing the heterozygotic state of the genes.

However, you also wish to produce extreme expression in terms of the mask or throat spots, as well as in the placement and markings on the wings, especially in given varieties. To achieve this, you need to retain the heterozygotic state, at least until these desirable features have been acquired in your stock. Once this has been achieved, the objective is to fix the extremes into the stock, whilst retaining all of the medium features.

The problem with extreme features is that they are harder to come by — they are spread in the population. Were this not so, all breeders would have outstanding birds for these. Some features may be controlled by a relatively small number of genes, others may be subject to the influence of many modifiers that are not easily gathered together. There is thus a time factor to be considered. There is also the possibility that some of the desirable genes may be linked to others that are undesirable, either phenotypically or physiologically. The ways in which you might overcome your dilemma are the subject of the rest of this chapter, and the basis of what breeding is all about.

LIKE-TO-LIKE PAIRINGS

Many budgerigar breeders adopt a system based on like-to-like matings, which usually means best to best. However, whilst a degree of success is possible, it is rarely of substance. This is because the genes that create a given phenotype in one bird may not be the same as those that produced a similar appearance in another. A simple example to illustrate the point would be in respect of mimic genes, as in fallows. Pairing an English and Scottish fallow together, which is like to like, will produce normals.

Clearly, if two birds are similar in appearance, there is a chance that the offspring may resemble the parents. This is because, unlike major color mutations, which have a simple action, features of the body as a whole are

An indoor aviary. Budgies are colony breeders: the company of fellow budgies stimulates their interest in reproduction.

controlled by many genes in the heterozygous state. When two similar birds are paired, there is every chance that this may bring together some of these polygenes and thus increase the chances that the chicks will resemble one or other of the parents. Such matings may improve the uniformity of a population, if accompanied with rigid selection, but such stock will not have prepotency when it is paired with stock that is more homozygous. Like to like in terms of physical appearance is therefore not to be confused with like to like in relation to the genes that create that appearance.

UNLIKE TO UNLIKE

This is sometimes referred to as compensatory pairing. Generally, this form of breeding will increase the heterozygotic state of the offspring. It will often produce stock of a more uniform state than the extremes of the parents, but such uniformity is likely to be short lived. By the next generation, the extremes are likely to reappear. Further, you may not get the intermediate you planned on. If a bird is undersized, for example, then the best course is to pair it with a bird that is ideal for its size, as this will minimize the potential variation within the offspring.

When compensatory matings have been undertaken, it should not be assumed they have achieved the objective at the first generation, even if this appears to have been the case. The offspring must still be paired to birds of ideal size so that further minimization of potential variation is strengthened. All breeders use unlike-to-unlike pairings in a sense because they will obviously be trying to select for improvement of given features. The method can therefore be viewed in specific or in general terms: it is in the latter that you must exercise the most caution.

INBREEDING

Because of its connotations with abnormalities, many breeders will not inbreed their stock. By not so doing, they deny themselves many benefits of this system of breeding. It is true that the system does carry with it certain risks, but these are often blown out of all proportion. Let us review

Inbreeding, which is the mating of closely related birds, requires careful thought and planning.

inbreeding in its genetic implications rather than in hand-me-downs that are based on a lack of understanding of what the truth is.

The first thing that should be said is that inbreeding has never created an abnormality. What it does do is raise the possibility that if there is one present in the stock, it will more quickly become apparent than if random breeding is practiced. Consider the following situation. A given major defect is created by the recessive *a* gene that has a very low incidence in the population. Most birds are therefore AA for that feature. Any bird that is *aa* is culled or not bred from. The gene can thus circulate only through A*a* birds. In the vast majority of instances, these birds will only ever meet AA birds, so 50% of the offspring will be AA, and 50% A*a*. By this means the incidence of the defect remains at a low level. However, if a breeder then commences an inbreeding program, and happens to have one A*a* bird, this will quickly spread the gene to others in the program. It will not take long before a pair of A*a* birds are paired and the result will be a 25% chance of producing *aa*, and a 50% chance of producing A*a*. There will also be a 25% chance of producing AA birds. The AA birds, regardless of how intensively they are inbred,

can never yield an *aa* chick, so inbreeding *per se* has not created the problem; it has merely brought it to the surface.

If the breeder perseveres with the program and culls all *aa* stock, the result will be a steady decline in the A*a* birds and a corresponding increase in the AA stock. Ultimately, the frequency of the *a* gene will be lower than in the average of the population. If the breeder commenced with only AA birds, then the defect will never occur at all because, unlike in the general population, it will not even be in existence in that stock.

Inbreeding will increase the homozygous state of your stock, providing selection is made from the offspring. This is important because it is often stated that inbreeding creates greater uniformity, which is not true. If your stock is A*a* for a feature and you pair it to a similar genotype, you will create AA, Aa and aa — three phenotypes where only one was present at the start, even though you have increased the homozygosity of the stock in two of these types. Uniformity will only come by selecting for AA or aa, whichever is the more desirable.

If you commence with AA and aa stock, then you are practicing unlike to unlike, which is not inbreeding and, of course, will result in raising the heterozygous state of the stock, at least initially and until you begin to inbreed.

It is perhaps a timely point to define inbreeding in order to establish when a line is not inbred. The best definition of inbreeding is the mating together of individuals that have a closer relationship to each other than the average of the population. This means that it is possible for stock to be regarded as inbred in one area or country, but not in another. When a new mutation is in its early years of establishment, it follows that the degree of inbreeding is necessarily higher than in the average of the budgerigar population as a whole.

Generally, breeders will tend to regard inbreeding as the mating of father to daughter, son to mother, and sibling matings — brother to sister. They may consider cousin matings either inbreeding or close breeding. Once the relationship is more distant, this is usually referred to as line-breeding, but the distinction is opinion rather than precise. It is simply inbreeding at a more dilute level.

The object of inbreeding is clearly the fixation of desirable genes. The closer the inbreeding, the quicker will fixation take place — as long as judicious selection is practiced. The problem is that there is no way of telling which unwanted genes are either linked to the desired features or are in recessive form and will become both fixed and visual as the inbreeding of virtues takes place. Furthermore, once features are homozygous, the effects of selection will have less impact, or none at all.

This may limit you in further improvements if you did not start with birds that had the most desirable genes in the first place. Likewise, it limits your ability to remove faults. This would suggest that the path to take is a less intense form of inbreeding (linebreeding) that retains a reasonable degree of heterozygosity in your stock, thus allowing you more flexibility to remove faults, whilst gathering desired genes together. It is obviously a longer process, but any system will take a number of years to show its merits if it is based on a steady move towards homozygosity.

Linebreeding entails the selection of a given quality bird and then breeding to it via birds that are related to it, but not closely. By this method it is hoped that there will be a steady increase in the number of homozygous genes from that bird. It is obviously better if the bird to be bred to is of a high breeding standing with known homozygosity for certain traits. If it is just a good-looking bird, it is pure chance whether or not you will obtain the genes that created those good looks.

The question of inbreeding drawbacks should be discussed.

Inbreeding can be problematic because undesirable characteristics of the intended pair can be magnified and passed on to the offspring.

Negative effects are certainly evident in a number of exhibition-budgerigar breeder's birdrooms. Many traits, such as egg production, hatchability, parental ability, disease resistance, and sterility, are created on a build-up basis by polygenic recessive genes. As you inbreed, you increase the chances of these coming together, or not doing so. They may be linked with features that you find pleasing, but which may be deleterious to the bird. Or, they may not be, or it may be that some are and some are not. There is no way of knowing what the situation will be until you meet it; it appears to differ from one species to the next. In the first quarter of this century, much research was done on the inbreeding of rats (King) and guinea pigs (Wright). The rats were inbred, brother to sister, for over 25 generations. The conclusions were that, if anything, vigor, disease resistance, and fertility were stronger than in the average of the population. In guinea pigs the results showed a movement both ways. Some lines were less healthy and productive compared to the average, others were marginally more so — this was over 23 generations. In both cases, the majority of problems occurred in the first few generations. Thereafter, lines either quickly perished or they prospered. Throughout these experiments thousands of individuals were bred — well beyond the capabilities of the average hobbyist. Selection was a vital part of the program.

From this brief look at inbreeding drawbacks, one can possibly draw conclusions as to the problems facing British breeders in particular. With very few fresh gene lines being imported into the country for many years, most of the top exhibition stock is inbred to a higher degree than is common in, say, mainland Europe or the USA. When inbreeding is practiced on this stock, problems will tend to show themselves rather quickly in many instances. This situation will only get worse unless breeders rigidly select for health, vigor, and fertility. Alas, this is not always done because there is still the strong temptation to breed from top show winners. A successful inbred line is not readily disbanded, even if it becomes obvious the line has problems in these areas.

Although the show birds in a given country may run into many thousands, one should not lose sight of the fact that many of these are closely related; they carry many of the same genes. Breeder A sells to B who produces stock that is sold to C and D. These may go back to B for additional stock as well as to A. In turn they sell to other breeders who likewise may go to A,B,C, and D. Now, if the original birds were homozygous for traits such as vigor, number of eggs, or a desired physical feature, there should be no problems as long as each breeder selects for these features.

An opaline olive cock. Hybridization, the pairing of two different varieties or species, can be employed to strengthen or improve a line of stock.

However, if the original stock was already moving towards a decline in inbred quality, then this steady breeding back to it will probably be increasing the polygenes that will create problems. Here we see the vital need not to assess a bird purely on its visual appearance, outstanding as this may be. You should examine records on all hereditary traits — especially those concerned with health and reproduction.

HYBRID VIGOR

This term is applied to the result of crossing two distinct species, or even varieties. It is genetically called heterosis. It results, often, in offspring that are bigger than either of the parents, constitutionally more vigorous, more resistant to disease, and with greater fertility. However, after the first generation, the advances made begin to fall back. It is postulated that the inbred lines each hold many genes in linked groups that are dominant for desirable traits. When these meet up with the pure recessives in the opposing inbred line, they obviously result in a heterogeneous situation — so the dominant traits show themselves. As it is a two-way situation, many of the undesirable genes are masked. Clearly, this assumes the dominants are at differing loci to those in the other inbred line. It can, of course, mean that inbred lines do not display heterosis, but it seems they often will.

The benefit of this practice is that if inbred lines are cross-paired, it can introduce the needed vigor to a line. If the two lines are closely related anyway, there may be minimal disturbance to the homozygosity of many features. This is because with inbred lines you do have a good idea of which genes are likely to be in a homozygous state. This may not be the case with random outcrossing. Of course, you must remember the point made about similar-looking birds not having the same genotype, even if the lines are related.

Another benefit of outcrossing inbred lines is that you just might produce some outstanding birds. Consider the two birds in this pairing: AABBccddEEFFGG x AAbbCCDDeeFFgg = AABbCcDdEeFFGg. One parent bird was outstanding in five features, the other in four. The offspring carry seven of the features, though five of these are in a heterogeneous state. Nonetheless, the inbred lines may gain from this situation. They may have overcome much of the

When setting breeding goals, it is necessary to consider vigor and soundness as important as physical appearance.

problems discussed, and have introduced the two needed genes C and D to one line and B,E, and G to the other. By careful selection it should be possible to bring these to the pure state over a period of time. Of course, this is a rather simplified example, but it does illustrate the point being made.

The note of caution is that on seeing such improved birds, many a breeder might be tempted to abandon his or her inbred line in favor of the outcross. This would probably be a major error because it would take a long while to reestablish the homozygous state of the stock. The wiser move would be to retain the outcross as part of the inbred line already established.

CLOSING THOUGHTS

The object of any good breeder should be to increase the overall quality of the stock, not simply to produce the odd show winner from amongst a sea of mediocrity. Any unskilled breeder could achieve the latter with no real problem, assuming they purchase some decent birds at the outset. It is not enough, however, to raise the quality of the birds purely in the visual sense. They must be vigorous both in their constitution and in their breeding performance. If they are not they are worthless, other than as show birds if they are to this standard.

If you practice any form of inbreeding, you must make selections based on the individual, never on the mass.

Exactly when you commence inbreeding and when you move back to a more dilute form only you can decide. Do not outcross at all unless this is to achieve a very fixed objective. If there are no problems, then routinely outcrossing every few generations has nothing to recommend it and every reason not to do it.

Exhibition

The exhibition side of the budgerigar fancy is both fascinating and highly competitive. For many, it is the logical conclusion to their breeding programs, for some the reason they breed in the first place, and for others purely a social meeting place where friendships are formed with those who share the same interests. Not every breeder is prepared to subject their birds to the rigors of a show season, yet such people will enjoy visiting shows to see the quality of birds on display and maybe to buy a bird or two. At the major exhibitions there will be many trade booths selling specialized equipment, seed, and every conceivable item that might remotely interest the birdkeeper.

I would wholeheartedly recommend that you visit a

Even if you are not interested in showing your birds, attending a budgie exhibition will be enjoyable and educational.

For the avid show enthusiast, nothing is more exciting than to have his budgerigar take top honors in a competition.

BUDGERIGA...

...nd BEST BEGINNER...

/65

G. N. Hillier & Sons Ltd., Printers, Bus...

PAISLEY & DISTRICT BUDGERIGAR SOCIETY SPECIAL AWARD

number of shows, regardless of whether or not you wish to become a breeder, an exhibitor, or simply a pet budgie owner. I feel sure you will enjoy the experience, especially if you visit a large show.

TYPES OF SHOW

In the early years of the budgerigar fancy, these birds were exhibited as foreigns. Today, they are a fully domesticated species and thus not regarded as foreign birds. You can still see them in such bird shows, however, as the latter will invariably put on classes for budgies. They help to draw the public, and their entry fees help to make the show a success.

The smallest shows are those staged by local branches of the main budgerigar society of a country, or by local cage-bird societies. These are very informal affairs where there will not be large entries. They are excellent places for beginners to gain experience and to meet local members. At such events, breeders usually have a little more time to discuss things with the novice. The same is true of the judges, who are not darting here and there as they are in the large venues where they are kept real busy.

Rather larger than club shows are the open shows. Non-members can exhibit at these. There will be more classes scheduled and more birds on view. The largest of the specialty budgie shows will be those staged by the national budgerigar society of your country. These will bring together the best birds in the nation. At the 1990 Budgerigar Society show in England there were some 5,227 birds on view! Many of the major cage-bird exhibitions will also feature a large section devoted to budgerigars. These shows are very much a spectacle because they cater to all cage birds. You can see parrots, canaries, finches, and exotic softbilled birds, and there are invariably classes for talking birds, which of course will include budgerigars. The shows are advertised in the avicultural magazines.

JUDGING

Budgerigars are judged against a standard of excellence, which is determined by the national club of the country. The standard allocates points to various parts of the bird, as well as to the color and markings. These may differ slightly according to the color, but points for the general conformation, or type, are the same for any color. In Great Britain, judging is conducted behind closed doors, but in the USA it is done in front of the public and exhibitors alike, and adds much to the excitement of the occasion.

THE CLASSES

The number of classes scheduled by a given show is determined by the potential number of entries likely to be received. There is little point in having classes for every color variety if many of these will only attract one or two entries! A small show will therefore group colors together, whereas the largest exhibitions will have a class for nearly all colors and specific marking types (such as Spangles). Those that are new varieties, or poorly supported colors, will be grouped as Any Other Color (AOC). There are classes for cocks and hens and classes for the status of the breeder, such as beginner, novice, intermediate, breeder, champion, and so on. Whilst most classes are for single birds, there are nonetheless team classes. These will cater for teams of birds (two, four, six, and so on). The object is to present a team of exhibits that are as well matched as possible to each other in size and color.

The full workings of exhibition rules and structure is complex and varies from one country to another. If this side of the hobby appeals to you, you should contact your nearest budgerigar society branch and apply to be a member. You will then receive all of the information on how the system works, together with a copy of their monthly newsletter or magazine, as the case may be. At a show, the class winners for each sex compete for the best of that variety, and these go on to compete, ultimately, for the best bird in show and the best opposite sex.

PRIZES

Prize money, if offered at all, is rarely very much. It is not likely to cover the cost of your participation in a show unless you take the supreme honors. You may receive certificates or ribbons and maybe a cup or other trophy. There may also be 'specials' donated by individuals, by clubs, or by companies. These may be restricted to certain groups

of birds, or to the members of given clubs. Such awards may be in the form of trophies, seed, books, or even cash.

THE SHOW CAGE

Budgerigars are always exhibited in a standard show cage, which must meet the criteria laid down by the ruling society. The cage is painted black with white on the inside. The floor is covered with seed. There is a round door in the side and a handle on the top of the cage. The reason all cages must be identical is so

the judge will have no idea which bird is owned by whom.

No marks or other means of cage identification are permitted. Only the number label is allowed to be placed onto the cage. This identifies the owner and is known only to the owner and the officiating stewards. The cage must be kept in immaculate condition and repainted whenever it begins to look faded. A poor looking cage could cost an exhibitor a place amongst the winning birds. Cages can be transported in specially made carry boxes designed to take two or more cages.

ENTERING A SHOW

When a show is advertised, it will give the

To obtain information about budgie standards and exhibitions, contact the national budgerigar association for the area in which you live.

closing date for entries. You must write to the secretary for a schedule of classes and an entry form. This must be filled in and returned, along with appropriate fees, to the secretary by the date stated. The entries will be acknowledged, and labels will be supplied for your use on the show cage. It is important that you fill in the entry form with care. If you make a mistake and enter a bird for a class it is found ineligible for, it is not judged and you lose your fee. You must also be sure you are entered for any specials that you are entitled to compete for. If this is overlooked, you may miss such awards and maybe see them go to a bird that your bird had already beaten!

SHOW TRAINING

It is very important that your budgerigars are well trained so they will stand on the show perch in a bold manner. Many a good bird has missed out on a win or place because it shrank into the corner of the cage when being judged. Show training can never begin too early in the bird's life. The winners not only show off their own qualities but are testimony to the many hours that the exhibitor has spent in training and preparing them.

The first training actually begins the minute a chick is handled. This commences the human's contact with the chick, which will help to ensure it has no fear of humans — very important in an exhibition bird. Once the chick is independent of its parents, it is placed in a stock cage. It can be very useful to arrange things such that a show cage is placed next to the stock cage. The stock cage side can have a round hole made in it so the chicks can enter

Banding, or ringing, a budgie serves as a means of identification. Normally, the band is encoded with the bird's hatching date, although some hobbyists also include data about the parent birds.

the show cage whenever they like. A favored tidbit, such as millet spray, can be placed in the show cage to encourage the youngsters into it.

In this way, the exhibition cage becomes an extension of the youngster's home. The next stage is to close the door of the show cage and leave the budgie in this for maybe one hour on the first occasion. Slowly, over the weeks, you increase the time the budgie spends in its show cage until it thinks nothing of staying some

hours in it — ultimately overnight as well.

Whilst this stage is proceeding, you must also place the show cage in differing positions in the birdroom so the potential exhibit becomes quite familiar with seeing differing birds opposite to it. You can then take it into your home and 'stage' it, as will be done at an exhibition. Friends can stop and look into the cage just as will happen at the show. It is also of value to wear glasses, or hats and overcoats — anything that the bird is unfamiliar with. Judges come in all shapes, sizes, and appearance, so you do not want your exhibit to dive for the nearest corner because it is suddenly confronted with a lady judge that has a gaudy feather sticking out of her hat as she evaluates the merits of your bird!

You must obviously ensure that your bird receives ample exercise and the best of foods so that it is a real fine example of fitness. As the show date draws closer, you should avoid handling the bird if possible so there is no risk of feathers being lost or damaged. Any that are damaged should be pulled out in the hope that they will be replaced in time for the show. The feathering will certainly benefit from receiving a regular mist spray, and the bird will enjoy this.

In the final days before the show, you may need to carefully remove any excess mask spots so that only the required number remain — six, and ideally large and placed as required by the standard. It should be stressed that exhibits really

A budgie in the process of being banded.

must be ready for a show because all too often judges will comment on the number of birds that were out of condition. Sometimes, however, it is not so much that this state exists but simply that the bird is ill prepared for the physical exertion that is involved in the transportation and general preparation that precedes being judged. By this time, it does not look at its best. Some birds are good 'stayers,' others fade quickly during long outings away from home.

TRANSPORTING THE EXHIBITION BIRD

You may decide to personally take your bird to the show, or you may have an arrangement with a friend who will take yours with his or hers. Clubs will often arrange communal transport, or you may freight the bird to a show

via rail or road. Freighting is not the best way to transport birds and should be avoided. It is beneficial that your bird arrives in plenty of time to be staged but not so early that it will be spending unnecessary time in its cage awaiting judging. When shows are spread over two days, the birds are tended by the exhibition stewards, and the venue must provide adequate heat and ventilation for the birds throughout the period of the show and its setting up.

AFTER THE SHOW

The exhibits are required to remain in the staging area until a given time on the final day of the show. This is because the paying public quite naturally expect to see all of the birds that were entered. Rarely, you might obtain an early removal pass, but these are harder to come by these days because

Keep in mind that shows can be stressful to any kind of bird. When you return from a show, give your pet plenty of time to rest up, particularly if you intend to use it for breeding purposes.

is wise to place the birds in an isolation cage because a bird show is obviously a high-risk area in terms of containing stock that might be incubating an illness. (Show visitors as well might be carrying germs.)

The show cage should be thoroughly disinfected, rinsed, and placed in a polyethylene bag or its like so it is ready for the next show (but it should be cleaned again before being used). It is because of the health risk and the physical strain exhibiting places on birds that many breeders will not exhibit. You should not expect a show bird to commence the breeding season until it has had plenty of time to rest and recover its full vigor.

some years ago things got a little out of hand and people were turning up to find half the birds missing!

When you return home, it

You can appreciate that exhibiting birds really can be both costly and tiring, so it should be entered into on a gradual basis.

The Pet Budgerigar

Although many readers who have purchased this book will no doubt be concerned with keeping budgerigars from an aviary and breeding standpoint, nonetheless, for completeness, the pet bird should be discussed. In its appearance, the average pet budgie is quite removed from its show-cage counterpart. It is somewhat smaller, has a smaller skull, and its colors will not usually be quite so stunning. This does not mean they are not striking, simply that the pick of the best will have been retained by breeders or sold to others wanting to breed.

The throat spots of a pet bird will usually be smaller and less well placed than in the exhibition bird. Although much depends on the 'line' from which a budgerigar has come, the

A budgie that doesn't measure up to the standard can still make a fine pet.

pet bird bred from non-exhibition stock will typically live a little longer than that from inbred lines, but much will depend on how well it is accommodated and cared for.

AGE TO PURCHASE

The ideal age to obtain a pet budgerigar is when it is about 5 to 6 weeks old. At this time, it will be feeding independently of its parents. It will be much more suscep-tible to human imprinting at this age rather

A young budgie should not be taken from its parents before the age of about six weeks, at which time it will no longer be dependent on them.

than if it is an older bird. This said, even adult birds can be readily tamed,

though you will need to spend a little more time at this than with a youngster. Once a bird has developed its adult plumage, at about five months of age, it becomes very difficult to say how old it is.

If it contains a closed metal ring on its leg, then this is proof of its age. Rings are placed on chicks when they are only a few days old. After this time they will not fit over the feet. The rings carry a year date on them. If the bird has no rings and is in full plumage, then you really have to rely on the honesty of the seller to tell you the age. You can expect a pet budgie to live for about 7 to 9 years, but many have lived well past ten if they are of good constitution and contented.

WHERE TO PURCHASE

For a pet bird you can do no better than visit your local pet or bird shop. They will have a good selection of popular colors. If you

You can verify the age of your budgie by checking the date on its band. If your intended pet is unbanded and in full feather, it will not be possible to determine its exact age.

especially want a bird with a specific color or wing markings, then you should enquire if there are any local breeders of these in your area — maybe one of your friends may know. Alternatively, visit a local foreign bird or budgerigar show, where you will most certainly meet such a breeder, or at least one that can put you in touch with such a color specialist. You will find that most young stock will become available in the spring and summer months, as this is the peak breeding period. However, some will be bred indoors during the winter months, though these are not always as strong as birds bred when the weather is suited to this.

COCK OR HEN?

The cock bird will make the better pet on several accounts. Firstly, it is the more likely of the two sexes to learn to mimic words; secondly, it has the weaker bite. The latter should not, however, be a problem with a young bird. If you decide to have more than one pet, the cocks will get on better with each other than will hens. Of course, a cock and a hen will be very happy with each other. Both sexes will make delightful pets. As it is never wise to purchase any parrot with the assumption it will learn to talk, the choice of sex is not really a major factor you need worry unduly about.

ONE OR MORE BUDGERIGARS?

While it is true that many people keep just a single bird, I think two or even more is a much better proposition. These birds are extremely social in their wild state, so to deprive them of their own kind always seems a little sad.

When you are away from home they will greatly appreciate a companion. This will not necessarily detract from their affection for you as is sometimes stated. It may well reduce their potential talking ability, but this is a small price to pay for all the benefits gained both by the birds and by yourself.

ON ARRIVAL HOME

Once you have decided to purchase a budgerigar, it is always better to arrange its accommodation in advance of its arriving in your home. Collect the bird as early in the day as possible so it has plenty of time to settle into its cage before the evening. The food and water pots should be filled so it can sample these whenever it wants. Once placed into its cage, you can leave it for a while to explore the cage and study its new surroundings.

The cage should be placed where it is free from drafts, so opposite a door is not a good place. Try to keep the cage away from radiators, as these will tend to create fluctuations in the immediate area around them. This is one thing that may cause your pet to contract chills. The site should be such that it receives some sunlight but never such that the budgerigar cannot escape this whenever it wants to.

Your pet will appreciate being in a place where it can watch what is going on around it. It will also prefer

Keeping a large collection of budgies is a considerable responsibility involving time and money on your part. For the beginner budgie-keeper, it is best to start out with just one or two birds.

to be at a height that is reasonably level with your own eyes when you look into the cage. Birds prefer high vantage points and can become stressed if their cages are too low to the ground, as they feel insecure when anything passes them.

CHILDREN AND BUDGERIGARS

Children just love budgies, but they do not always appreciate how easily the birds can be frightened. You must instruct children not to run and jump around near the bird's cage, nor to frighten it by banging on the cage or by pushing things through the bars. Once the young bird has been hand-tamed,

Training a budgie is not that difficult. Much depends on the time and effort that you devote to your pet.

you can let the children hold it and they will really enjoy this. Do drill them never to leave doors or windows open when the pet is free flying in the room, nor to ever let your dogs and cats, if you have these, to be alone with the bird when it is out of its cage.

DANGERS IN THE HOME

Your home holds many potential dangers to a pet

budgerigar once it is allowed out of its cage. Some of those discussed may not be applicable to you, but check on all others, as one lax moment on your behalf could prove fatal to your cherished pet.

1. Open doors. If an outside door is left open, your pet may fly past you and away. The chances of it returning are, at best, very slim. Its own chances of survival are about on the same par.

2. Chimneys. Be sure any open fireplace is protected by a mesh guard. Your pet might badly burn itself if the fire was alight, or it may fly up the opening if there was no lighted fire.

3. Fish tanks. These should be covered with a canopy — this is, in any case, an advantage for the aquarium.

4. If you have an open living room/kitchen arrangement, be real sure none of the burners are alight when the pet is free. Likewise, be careful that no pans of hot liquids or foods are on a burner, even if the burner is not lit.

5. Ventilation and ceiling fans. Both of these could injure or kill your pet.

6. Irons. Be aware that a tame budgerigar might attempt to land on an iron if you were using this. Clearly, it could be badly burned in so doing.

7. Cats and dogs. Never leave these pets alone with your budgerigar when it is out of its cage. Even if they come to ignore it most of the time, there may always be the one time they get overexcited and snap or claw at it in play.

8. Windows. Glass is probably a material your pet has never encountered before. Many a pet bird has either killed itself or been

On occasion, your budgie may refuse to return voluntarily to its cage. It is a good idea to keep a bird net handy so that you are prepared for such occurrences.

badly injured when attempting to fly through it! If you can arrange to hang something over windows during your pet's initial flights around the room, this will prevent any risk of injury. If mesh curtain is used, be aware that the bird may become entangled in this (avoid it if possible).

9. Plants. Budgerigars will nibble away on any house plants. If these are poisonous, they could also cause it many problems. It is best to remove any that you might have doubts about or that you do not want destroyed.

10. Ornaments. Although ornaments may not be a direct danger to your pet, you may not be overjoyed if 'Joey' happens to land near one and, in panic, flutters and knocks it off a shelf. Knowing this is a possibility, it would be wise to remove any treasured and breakable items from shelves.

FINGER TAMING

If you have obtained a young bird, then finger taming is no problem at all.

Very often, straight-from-the-nest babies are already tame to this degree. Place your hand slowly into the cage once your budgerigar has had time to settle down. It may back away from it, but extend it so your index finger is just below its chest, slightly above its legs. Now gently move the finger upwards and against the youngster. It will step onto your finger. It may use its beak to take hold of your finger, but this is rarely a bite. Parrots use their beak rather like a third foot — to test that which they are going to hold on to.

A finger-tame youngster. Some budgies enjoy having the back of their head stroked while they are being held.

I would not let the budgie out of the cage for another day or so and until it will readily step onto your finger. This is very much a matter determined by how steady the bird is. Some are very tame within an hour of your commencing. When you are ready to let it out, simply open the cage door and it will find the

Above and Below: Taming a budgie. Your first goal will be to have your pet become accustomed to your hand in his cage. Each time you do this, move your hand closer to the bird. Eventually, he will come to perch on your hand.

opening. Initially, it will fly around in a bit of a panic, but you should just settle down in a chair and let it explore.

After a while, you can approach it to see if it will step onto your finger. If it is above your head height, do remember that your finger must always be positioned so it can step up — birds do not like to step down. Sometimes the bird will fly back to its cage of its own choice. It is more likely to do this if the cage is a home and not a prison. This means the more freedom it has the less reason it will have not to go back to its cage. If you need to manually take hold of your pet, do approach it quietly and talk soothingly to it. Do not snatch at it, but try simply to grasp it in your hand such that its back is in your palm. This should not be needed in most instances. You can also dim the lights in a room, and the budgie will be less inclined to fly off.

Once a budgie is finger tame, it will happily land on your shoulder, head, or outstretched hand. From this point onwards, everything gets much easier, and you will be able to stroke it, and even hold it if you work up to this very gently. If you have obtained an older budgerigar that is not already tame, you use the same methods. However, do understand it will take more patience because the budgie will be much more nervous than a bird just a few weeks old.

TALKING

You should regard a talking budgerigar as a bonus. Very often your pet will learn a few words without having received any form of instruction. If you do want to try teaching it, this should be done when no one else is in the room. There should be no distractions, such as the TV, radio, or even other pets, around. The evening is often

Once your budgie learns to perch calmly on your hand, he can be taken out of the cage to other areas in your home.

a good time because your pet will be getting a little tired and will be more receptive to listening to you.

Words should always be short, as should lessons — say five minutes initially and building up to no more than 15 minutes. However, your pet could receive two such lessons over the day. Try to make them at the same time each day, maybe one in the morning and the other at night, so a regular routine is established.

The budgerigar's potential vocabulary is on par with that of any of the parrots, and more than most. Do not expect a clear voice: this is only a little bird and the sound is high pitched and squeaky. The larger the parrot the more audible the sounds are. Very often, a budgie is limited more by its trainer than its ability. You must persevere. Once the first words are learned, you should continue to develop from that point — you have by then overcome the hardest part.

The first signs that your pet is attempting to mimic you is when you hear sounds that are a little different than its normal voice. This should encourage you.

When your pet can say

A challenging aspect of budgie-keeping is teaching your pet to talk. Lessons should take place in a quiet area, and they should be kept short. Whatever you do, don't expect too much too soon!

maybe ten or so words, you can then progress to the conditioned response. You can teach it to say 'very good thank you' and later 'how are you.' Once the budgie associates your approach to the cage with the question of 'How are you feeling?' it will give its reply. By this means you can build up quite an amazing dialogue. Budgies can be taught short verses of poetry as well. Of course, they may sometimes transpose words or sentences and may learn some of your lines as well: they will ask the question and then answer it all by themselves!

You may hear from other people that they have a better way of teaching a bird to talk than that given here. If this method is failing, then you have nothing to lose trying another, assuming you have been patient with your budgerigar. However, all methods come back to the essential need of a one-to-one situation with you and the bird and your being repetitive. Your pet learns 'parrot fashion' and applies no reasoning faculty to the subject.

TOYS

Your pet will enjoy playing with a whole range of toys, which can be found at your local pet shop. Other favorite items will often be small twigs from fruit trees, which will be both eaten and reduced to shreds. They are thus excellent for your bird as they help keep the beak in trim and occupy the bird for long periods of time.

SPRAYING

It is entirely probable that your pet will spend most, if not all, of its life in your home. This being so, you should bear in mind that in the wild state its plumage would, from time to time, receive a soaking when it rained. This helps to keep the feathers in good condition because the bird will carefully preen itself following such rains. The pet bird is often in a continual state of 'soft molt,' meaning its feathers are being continually shed and replaced, rather than their being molted out over a short period as is normal. This is no real problem, but it can be helpful if you spray your pet with tepid water once a week.

This little shower will be greatly enjoyed. The budgie will hang upside down and open its wings — so it has a real good time. It will then settle down and have a good preen. Do remember it should receive a spray, not a hosing down! On nice, warm summer days its cage can be placed outside if there is a short shower. Be sure that it has plenty of

Your budgie's antics with his toys will amuse and entertain you for hours on end. (Don't forget to clean toys and other cage equipment regularly.)

time to dry out before it goes to sleep for the night. Do not leave the budgie out in the sun for long periods where it has no shade to retreat to. It can suffer as badly as you can from the sun's rays if overexposed.

VACATIONS

Many budgerigar owners will go on vacation only to places where they can take their pets, but if you are unable to do this, then the next best thing is to have a friend come to your home every day and spend a few minutes attending to the bird. Alternatively, you may decide to let them look after it in their own home, which means it will have company. Pet stores sometimes offer a boarding service.

The more time you spend observing your budgie during his daily activities the better you will be able to discern when he is not feeling well.

Maintaining Health

Budgerigars, like yourself or any other organism, can fall ill to an enormous range of diseases. Many can be successfully treated, others cannot. Most can be prevented with good husbandry techniques. In this chapter, the emphasis is on prevention and the understanding of disease, but a number of major problems are detailed and the normal method of treating them given. One of the problems that faced the bird owner not so many years ago was that the cost of veterinary treatment was greater than the value of the bird. As a result, home diagnosis and treatment was the norm. The effect of export bans on many types of birds, especially parrots, was that their value rose significantly. It then became worthwhile to have them professionally treated. This resulted in an upsurge of research into avian diseases specific to these birds (as opposed to the previous situation, which was based on data applicable to poultry and game birds). Many vets started to specialize in the problems of cage and aviary birds.

It is still true that in many species, including budgies, the cost of treatment may exceed the value of the bird. It is a case of viewing such treatment from one of two viewpoints. If you have a cherished pet budgie, you will not relate its initial cost to its value to you, so treatment is worthwhile. If you have an aviary of birds, then, while veterinary treatment on one or two birds may seem costly in ratio to the value of the birds, it may be a case that by such treatment you save the entire stock.

PATHOGENIC ORGANISMS

Pathogens, disease-causing organisms, are life forms as much as your budgerigar is. They attack and are attacked; they build up or lose colonies depending on the environmental conditions they are living under. They can build up resistance to that which attacks them, such as natural antibodies or modern drugs, or they can be killed or held in check by these. Life is a continuum of battles between these opposing factions. Your role is to keep the odds very much in favor of your budgie. This is done by understanding the conditions that favor the pathogens, which are as follows:

1. Disease bacteria can build up their numbers when your bird is stressed. This condition is not easily defined because what affects one bird may not do so to another. Overcrowding is a prime cause of stress, as is bullying. In aviary conditions, the bird causing the intimidation may not even be in the same aviary, but in an adjacent one.

Newly acquired birds are often in a stressed state because they have been taken from an environment they were familiar with and placed into a new situation. The journey itself to the new home can stress them, which is why it should be as quick as possible. A sudden change in the diet, seeing cats or dogs near an aviary, the landing on the flight by birds of prey, or even some nearby noises are all happenings that can affect your birds in a negative manner. They draw on energy above and beyond their physical needs, and the birds invariably do not eat as well as they should.

Stress is a subconscious fear, and the more fear an animal displays the less it will eat — the systems controlling digestion and coping with stress are antagonistic. Such a bird is more open to invasion by pathogens than one that is relaxed and contented. If you notice your bird(s) shows signs of fear and is not eating as you think it should, then you must consider whether something in the environment is creating this situation.

The mental state of a bird is not always given the consideration that it should be given. It will influence the bird's willingness to breed, as well as to eat.

2. Temperature. Bacteria have optimum temperature requirements, and these are usually within the warm to hot range. When these conditions are present, especially in the upper range, they tend to coincide with the fact that the bird is uncomfortable, maybe stressed. The answer is to try and control the upper temperature range so it does not get too hot. However, heat can also be beneficial in the upper range if a bird has become unwell. At such times, you will increase this to a higher-than-normal setting, and this may prove too high for many microorganisms.

3. Unclean Conditions. Pathogens can easily multiply when conditions are dirty, especially when the birds are overcrowded as well. You have a multiple situation involved. In some instances, the pathogens are transmitted via the droppings of other animals, such as mice, rats, wild birds, or aviary birds that are already ill. Fleas, lice, and other parasites can live in the debris, or in un-

cleaned crevices, and invade the bird. Their own parasitic activities on the bird create problems, which are doubled by the fact that the lesions they open provide a prime source for secondary infection by other bacteria or fungus. In overcrowded conditions, the disease can easily pass from one bird to another by direct transmission.

The answer is, of course, to ensure that cleanliness is always maintained to the highest level possible. This kills many of the pathogens, while those not killed are kept at a low level of population. Thus, they may not be sufficient to overcome the natural defense mechanisms of the bird.

Perches should be cleaned with a solution of water and disinfectant, then rinsed very well and dried before being put back into the cage or aviary. Natural branches should be discarded once the birds have striped the bark from them. Any cracked feeder containers should be replaced. Cage bars and aviary netting should be cleaned to remove any debris. Floors must be swept and, ideally, washed each day and certainly every few days.

Aviary floors should receive a hosing once a week. The frames to your aviary should be routinely checked and be treated with a wood preservative each year so they will not become home to any number of potential pathogens or their carriers. Food storage bins must have a lid on them so they are protected from contamination by flies or rodents. The food itself must always be fresh and clean — discard any you have a doubt about.

If you breed your birds, then the nest boxes must be

thoroughly cleaned at the end and beginning of each season, as well as during the season should you have been unfortunate to have suffered from mite or other parasitic invasion. Indeed, if you have been subjected to a major problem in the aviaries or birdroom, it is probably best to dispose of all furnishings and start afresh. The number of birds you keep should be controlled by the space available. It can be very easy to overcrowd, which does not always mean per aviary or cage but simply in the numbers kept in a given area. If you develop a large set-up, it may be better to have two birdrooms rather than one, even though this will clearly increase your costs. Should an epidemic hit your stock, this might minimize your losses to one of the birdrooms.

Be aware that the area around your aviaries is potentially a source of trouble. For example, piles of leaves, grass clippings, and the like can be home to many pathogens. They may not be in your garden, but what about your neighbor's? This is always a thorny problem to deal with, depending on how well you get on with the neighbor!

QUARANTINE

Most birdkeepers under-stand the need to quarantine stock to be added to their collection, yet somehow they will put this off for one reason or another and just release birds into aviaries. After all, the supplier main-tains very high standards, and you have never had problems before — but maybe the supplier hasn't either. There is always a first time, and that could be enough to wipe out some or even all of your stock.

Keep new birds as far from your aviaries as possible for about 14 days. This will be time enough for most problems being incubated to show themselves. It gives you the time to closely observe the birds and see that they are eating well. Quarantine cages or flights must be maintained to a very high standard of hygiene. Do not use these cages for isolation units when dealing with potentially ill birds; the two should be kept quite separate.

KNOW YOUR BIRDS

Your budgerigars cannot tell you when they are feeling unwell, so it follows that by the time clinical signs are observed the problem has a head start. Sometimes there will be no clinical signs and only by observation of behavior might you suspect a problem. The normally greedy eater suddenly shows little interest in a favored item. The normally active bird simply sits on a perch, or one of the birds seeks a quiet spot away from the others. The fecal matter may become more liquid than usual. All of these are signs you can appreciate only if you know your birds as a result of observing them individually. The best time to do this is when they are feeding. If you find you do not seem to have the time to devote to this 'bird watching,' this tells you to reduce the number of birds kept.

If you are not devoting time to your birds, this can greatly reduce your ability to discern abnormal behavior. If the birds are not totally relaxed in your presence, they may 'mask' a problem. For example, a bird sitting with fluffed up feathers may quickly take to the air or start to move about on seeing your approach. Thus, you do not notice its abnormal stance. To overcome this, should such a situation occur, observe the birds from a distance — maybe even using binoculars. Always remember that before and after handling any sick bird you must thoroughly scrub your hands. Better still, purchase some disposable surgical gloves.

DIAGNOSIS

Even if you have taken every precaution to safeguard your birds, there is always the time when one or more may become ill. You have reason to believe a bird is acting abnormally, or is showing the first signs of a problem — what should you do? The answer is to isolate the bird or birds and make notes on what you perceive in order that you or your vet may attempt a diagnosis. There are only a limited number of ways that a bird can display signs of illness, but there are very many diseases and conditions that your bird can suffer from. This means that the symptoms for many illnesses are necessarily the same. Some symptoms clearly indicate given conditions, others do not. If your budgie is scratching a lot and you can see a parasite on the bird, then obviously this is the probable cause of the trouble. On the other hand, if it has diarrhea, this could indicate a whole range of internal disorders and only a veterinarian could realistically hope to pinpoint the exact one. This might necessitate microscopy, so you will appreciate that home diagnosis is at best unreliable, at worst potentially fatal. The following is a list of some of the things you should make notes on.

1. When did you first notice the bird was not acting normally?

2. In what way(s) did this show itself?

3. How long have you had the bird?

4. Was it quarantined?

5. Was it eating and drinking well prior to its abnormal behavior?

6. Are any other birds showing similar symptoms?

7. When was the last bird owned by you ill?

8. Is the bird in a cage or aviary that has previously housed an ill bird?

9. Have you changed the diet of the bird lately?

10. Have you changed your seed supplier recently?

11. Do you have a problem with mice or rats in your aviary or birdroom?

12. Has the bird been attacked by another bird or animal?

13. Is the bird showing any clinical symptoms? If so, which?

14. What is the state of the bird's feces?

15. How fast is the bird deteriorating?

This data will be of great help to your veterinarian, and it is also valuable to you for your own breeding records. It will form part of a bird's history and may well indicate which cocks or hens are tending to pass on reduced health vigor to their chicks.

TREATMENT

The first treatment begins when you isolate the bird from all other livestock. If you are a breeder with a lot of birds, then it is definitely worth having some treatment facilities, such as a hospital cage. This can either be a commercial unit

Cross-sectional view of a nicely designed hospital cage. Whatever type of hospital cage you select, it must be equipped with a thermometer so that you can regulate the cage temperature. Too high or too low a temperature will stress the bird.

or one that you have fashioned yourself. If we are talking about a single pet budgerigar, then it is a case of improvising in order to try and achieve what is to be discussed.

If you make your own hospital cage, then you will need a wooden stock cage and an infrared lamp. The latter should have a thermostat so you can control the temperature. It should be the dull emitter type so it is not giving off a bright glare, as happens with spotlights. The glass should also be shatterproof. You can obtain special livestock models from avicultural supply specialists. These will come complete with clamps that can be attached to the cage bars.

The lamp should be sited to one side of center so the bird can move away from the heat if it so desires. With this in mind, place two perches in the cage and have these lower than normal. The temperature should be about 32°C(90°F). If this does not bring about an improvement within 48 hours, then it can be raised by 1 to 3°C. If the initial temperature appears to give the bird discomfort, then lower it slightly, as the risk of stress is counterproductive in an ailing bird. Water must be available at all times; a small dish of it, additional to the drinking water, will help to keep a reasonable humidity level in the cage. If an antibiotic is to be given, it may be added to the water. The alternative is a powder form sprinkled on the seed, but this is invariably a waste of powder because it is ignored by the bird. Adding the antibiotic to the water is not ideal because you have no control over how much the bird will take, but it is often your only option, given the small size of budgerigars.

You can obtain special stainless steel tubes and syringes for medicating budgies. These are the most effective way of administering antibiotics. The crucial aspect of their use is that they must never be forced down the bird's throat. As long as the bird is held correctly and no force is used, the risk of the tube harming the bird, or entering its windpipe, is almost nil. You should have your vet show you how to use the syringe.

If your bird has been placed in a hospital cage, then it should not be taken to the vet as the change in temperature would certainly make matters worse. Ask the vet to make a house call or take a detailed diagnosis sheet for the vet to study. It may be useful to also bring a sample of the bird's fecal matter.

RECOVERY

Once the patient is showing signs of recovery, do not on any account discontinue with the treatment prescribed by your vet: this will almost certainly result in a relapse — and further treatment may prove of no avail. Continue until the patient has fully recovered. At this stage you can then begin the crucial acclimatization process of slowly lowering the hospital cage temperature over a few days — until it is at room temperature. The bird can then be returned to its aviary or birdroom flight. However, do not return a bird to an outside flight during inclement weather. Keep it indoors until the weather improves.

DEAD BIRDS

Should one of your aviary birds suddenly die without displaying clinical signs of illness or fail to recover from treatment, you are advised to have an autopsy done on it. Your vet can arrange this. The cost of this will be more than repaid if it pinpoints a problem that might save many other of your birds. The dead body should be taken to the vet in a suitable container at the earliest opportunity. If it must be kept overnight in your home, then place the container in the refrigerator — not in the freezer. A post mortem may not always determine the cause because pathogens often leave the host as soon as it has died. If internal tissue has been wasted, this will at least be visible and might enable the vet to hazard a professional guess at the cause, thus be able to suggest a course of action to prevent further incidents in your stud.

SYMPTOMS AND TREATMENTS

The following are a selection of possible conditions that may be met with in budgerigars, together with their cause and suggested or likely treatment. If you wish to study more on the diseases of birds, then it is recommended that you obtain *Bird Diseases* by Arnall and Keymer, TFH Publications. This can be ordered through any good pet shop.

1. Bird scratches excessively. This usually indicates an external parasite, such as fleas, lice, or mites — usually the latter two. Fleas are easily seen with the naked eye, as they are very mobile. Lice are flattened and move slowly through the feathers at skin level. Mites are much smaller and not easily seen, but a flashlight in the roosting area at night may see masses of them scurrying for cover. Treatment is via proprietary sprays or powders. With fleas and mites it is essential that all cage furnishings are treated and retreated some days later. Scratching may also be the result of either a

This poor budgie has scaly face, French molt, and an undershot beak. Scaly face can be treated; French molt cannot. The beak should be trimmed.

nutritional deficiency or simple boredom, especially in caged birds.

2. Scaly face and leg. These two conditions are really the same, just affecting different parts of the body. The skin becomes encrusted with flake-like pieces of skin. These may become hardened into knobbly flakes. In bad cases the face looks terrible; the condition should never be allowed to develop to the state that is sometimes seen. The condition can be treated with modern remedies, and even painting with benzyl benzoate will effect a cure. Always carefully examine, using a hand lens, the beaks of newly acquired stock if they appear to be flaky or pitted with small holes.

3. French molt. This is a dreaded disease in budgerigars. It manifests itself in youngsters who molt excessively. If badly affected the birds are referred to as 'runners' by breeders. The cause of the condition is not known, but molters that are bred from tend to produce molters. It would seem that a number of factors contribute to the condition. Other than looking unsightly, molters appear none the worse in other health aspects. Do not breed any stock showing signs of the problem, and try to observe if situations causing stress can be found.

4. Bird plucks its feathers. There are numerous reasons why a bird will pluck its feathers, but even careful veterinary attention may fail to unearth the answer. The most obvious reason is boredom, followed by a nutritional deficiency, followed by a cellular physiological problem. Birds condemned to long periods in a cage will often resort to feather plucking,

the more so if they are single pets. Let them out more often, and spend more time talking to them. Maybe the diet is lacking in something. Give them a wider ranging diet. Try giving them some salt in a separate dish — this works wonders in some instances. If all else fails, and if your vet cannot find the answer, see if a friend will let you place the bird in his aviary for a while. Stress will prompt feather plucking.

5. Overgrown beak and nails. These situations are often seen in stock that is given no access to branches to chew on, and where the perches are too thin. The condition may also be found in poorly bred stock that has a genetic problem causing non alignment of the beak. The answer is to let your vet trim the beak and the nails. Never let your birds get into the sort of condition that is

Prevention of illness is easier to achieve than cure. One aspect of preventive maintenance is to keep your budgie's living area as clean as possible.

sometimes seen. This is the result of gross negligence.

6. Broken wings or limbs. There is very little you can do for a budgie that breaks its wings or a limb. Attempts to put splints on legs, or to strap up a wing, usually end up with the bird causing more damage by trying to remove these. The best way to deal with the problem is to isolate the bird in a cage with a very low perch. The wing or limb will repair itself but may thereafter be held in a somewhat abnormal position. In many cases the bird is none the worse for this; some however may not be able to fly very well if a wing break is bad.

7. Cuts and lumps. Small cuts will heal themselves. All you need do is to bath the area and smear on a suitable antiseptic cream or use a styptic pencil to stop the blood flow. Bad wounds should be referred to your vet. Likewise, all lumps that develop must be subject to veterinary scrutiny. Old budgies may develop non-benign tumors, but seem none the worse for these.

8. Loose droppings. This is a relative term. To know if it is applicable you must know what the normal droppings are like. The foods eaten will affect both the color and the viscosity of the fecal matter. If the condition persists and becomes accompanied by other clinical symptoms, then you should consult your vet, as clearly the bird has an internal problem and the diarrhea is merely the visible evidence of this. The problem may be no more than a chill or dietary upset, but in such instances it will rapidly clear up if the bird is isolated and subjected to hospital cage heat treatment.

9. Difficulty in breathing.

A white budgie cock. Check your budgie on a regular basis for any abnormalities such as cuts or lumps. The earlier a problem is detected the better the chance of effecting a cure.

If the bird is wheezing and gasps for air, then it likely has a respiratory problem. Consult your vet.

10. Going light. This is the term used to describe the condition when the breast bone is clearly evident. The problem is nutritional and is not easily overcome once it has been allowed to develop. The feeding regimen should be discussed with your vet or with a well established budgerigar breeder.

11. Worms. Some birds are infested with worms of some sort or another. These are not usually a problem and exist without any negative effect on their host. However, if they reach high levels, they can adversely affect your birds. Their numbers often rise when the bird is already unwell. To avoid the risk of them reaching infestation levels, it is essential that hygiene is of the highest order because it is by ingesting the eggs of the worms that their life cycle is completed. The eggs are passed via the feces of other birds or by the one that is already infested.

You can routinely administer powders or liquid vermicides onto the food, but this is usually not effective enough. The only sure way of administering the correct dose is via crop tubes: this is a time-consuming job if you have a lot of birds, but it is the only way to proceed if you are faced with the problem. Discuss the matter with your vet.

12. Weeping and inflamed eyes. This condition may arise from a localized infection, or it may indicate a more serious condition, such as chlamydiosis (formerly ornithosis or psittacosis). The latter can be

transmitted to humans. You must consult your vet in order to establish what the problem is; clearly the symptoms are typical of very many conditions. The application of an ointment or a liquid will cure a localized infection. Modern drugs such as tetracycline, which is a broad-spectrum antibiotic, will often bring about recovery of chlamydiosis if treatment is given early enough.

There are a number of conditions that may arise during the breeding season and that affect the hen, the egg, or both. In conclusion, you will appreciate that many diseases in budgerigars are directly a consequence of situations that you control — stock levels, cleanliness, nutrition, observation of the birds and prompt action once a problem is noted.

This budgie has bright clear eyes, which is one sign of good health. If your pet develops any problems with his eyes, check with your vet.

THE ATLAS OF PARROTS
By Dr. David Alderton
ISBN 0-86622-120-4
TFH H-1109
   In addition to being enjoyed for its beautiful full-color portrayals of *all* of the parrots of the world, this highly readable and practical book is the ultimate reference on parrot-keeping. Additionally, a complete checklist of parrot genera and species is provided. This book will be treasured by bird fanciers in general and parrot enthusiasts in particular.
   Hard cover, 544 pp., 10 x 14", over 300 full-color photos and drawings.

PARROTS OF THE WORLD
By Joseph M. Forshaw
ISBN 0-87666-959-3
TFH-PS-753
   Contents: This book covers every species and subspecies of parrot in the world, including those recently extinct. Information is presented on the distribution, status, habitats, and general habits. Almost 500 species and subspecies are illustrated in full color on large color plates.
   Hard cover, 584 pp., 9½ x 12½".
   Almost 300 large color plates depicting close to 500 different parrots; many line illustrations.

TAMING AND TRAINING PARROTS
By Dr. E. Mulawka
ISBN 0-86622-098-4
TFH-H-1019
   Contents: This book deals effectively with Dr. Mulawka's proven methods of successful parrot training. In this volume, which is heavily illustrated with both color and black and white photos, the author imparts his techniques for cultivating your pet parrot's innate abilities to learn.
   Hard cover, 5½x 8", 349 pp.
   152 full-color photos, 26 black and white photos.

TRAINING YOUR PARROT
By Kevin P. Murphy
ISBN 0-87666-872-4
TFH H-1056
   Contents: Introduction. The Pet Parrot In Your Home. Selecting Your Parrot. Housing and Equipment. Daily Care. Taming. Speech Training.
   Hard cover, 5½ x 8", 192 pp.
   Illustrated with full-color and black and white photos.

ENCYCLOPEDIA OF BUDGERIGARS
By Georg Radtke
ISBN 0-86622-734-2
TFH-1027
   Contents: Care and Breeding. Disease Prevention and Treatment. Care and Training of House Pets. Selective Breeding. The British Show Budgerigars. Color Varieties—Their Origin and Development.
   Hard cover, 5½ x 8", 320 pp., 148 full-color photos.

BUDGERIGAR HANDBOOK
By Ernest H. Hart
ISBN 0-86622-134-4
TFH-901
   Contents: Forming a Stud. Modes of Inheritance. Basic Breeding Techniques. The Mechanics of Breeding. Aviaries and Equipment. Feeding and Management. Selection and Upgrading. Trouble Hints and Ailments. Shows and The Standard. Matings and Color Expectation. Training The Pet Budgerigar. The Future.
   Hard cover, 5½ x 8½ ", 251 pp.
   104 color photos, 67 black and white photos.

Index